Presented To:

_____

From:

_____

Date:

_____

Perfect Love Heals

Healing Broken Hearts

Stuart DeVane

Perfect Love Heals

Published by Perfect Love Heals Ministries

ISBN 10: 0615934250
ISBN 13: 978-0615934259
Library of Congress Control Number: 2013922421
Perfect Love Heals Ministries, Oceano, CA

For worldwide distribution

Dedication

I dedicate this book to God the Father, Son, and Holy Spirit, Who love the brokenhearted and love to heal them all.

I dedicate this book to all of those who desire healing and are at a standstill and to all who have a passion to minister healing.

I dedicate this book to the church, the Bride of Christ, who Jesus redeemed with His own blood.

Endorsements

Perfect Love Heals really reveals the Father's heart toward those who need inner healing. Stuart focuses the compassion of God toward those who are broken and demonstrates how the Lord uses the Love anointing to unlock the hearts of those who are seeking to be set free. Stuart and Shereen are leaders at the Healing Rooms of the Santa Maria Valley, and we have witnessed many people completely healed, restored, and set free through their ministry. They not only teach on the power of Love, they truly are a living example of it.

Rick Taylor
International Association of Healing Rooms
Divisional Director of North America
President/Director of Healing Rooms of the Santa Maria Valley

After my personal assistant, David Kingsly, began to read this book, I knew immediately it was not another "self-help" book. Rather, I sensed it was a book about the heart, for the heart, and written from the heart. I know Stuart DeVane personally and highly recommend this book for anyone who desires to allow the perfect love of God and His Christ to heal their broken heart. If your heart is already healed, then read this book for its substance so when you come across a broken heart, you will have the tools in your arsenal. I have personally observed Stuart living out these truths. I give my full endorsement for *Perfect Love Heals* and only desire that all who read this book will walk out these truths written herein.

Papa Paul Cain
Paul Cain Ministries

You have hit the nail on the head! "His name is Jesus, Jesus. Sad hearts weep no more. He has healed the broken hearted, Opened wide the prison doors, He is able to deliver evermore."

Pastor Harry Goh
Founder of the Garden Community Church
Bakersfield, California

In his book, *Perfect Love Heals*, Stuart reveals the power of the Father's love. It shows the Father's heart in so many ways. Throughout each chapter, Stuart has captured the essence of love the way I believe the Father wants His children to experience love. Love truly does heal and mend broken hearts. Thank you, Stuart, for writing this wonderful book about such an important subject.

Ed Lixey
Founder of Jehu Ministries International

Acknowledgments

I want to thank my wonderful wife, Shereen, for helping me make the book more understandable! My sons, David and Daniel: thank you for regularly encouraging me and asking questions about this book. Pastor Harry Goh: thanks for spending countless hours mentoring me. Your life is full of the testimony of Jesus! Rick and Lori Taylor and the Healing Rooms and Apostolic Center of the Santa Maria Valley: thank you for all your love and encouragement – TEAM! You are AMAZING! You live what you teach and you do both well. Tina Smithson: special thanks for introducing me to healing the soul over 30 years ago.

Contents

Preface

My family and friends have been asking me consistently for the past 7 years, "When are you going to finish your book?" I am excited to be able to finally answer their question with "NOW" instead of my usual "hopefully soon." I believe I have rewritten this book at least four times. My only explanation for why it took so long is that I first needed to live it out. I have been ministering in the area of healing for the past thirty years, but now old things have passed away and I am living in the new things of God!

I have found that writing a book is actually easy; living out what you've written is a whole different matter. Yes, God's truth will always be TRUTH, no changing that, but living out His truth in healing the brokenhearted for the past seven years has caused my heart, soul, and mind to shift.

My relationship with Jesus began when I received His forgiveness, which was the healing of my spirit. Then I began to recognize and practice the truth of divine physical healing. Later, after reading a book a friend gave me, I became aware of healing the soul. I first received healing for my soul from Jesus and then soon after, became an assistant pastor. Now I have the privilege of being part of the Healing Rooms and Apostolic Center of Santa Maria, CA.

Using biblically-based principles is my approach to the ministry of healing the brokenhearted. These principles are the subject of the chapters of this book, including the cross, forgiveness, honesty with God and encounters with Jesus. Some other principles include the Kingdom of God, power and authority and pouring the goodness of God into people. Healing the brokenhearted is biblical, simple and transferable. Healing is designed to be ministered in the love of God.

My heart is overflowing with a good theme;
I recite my composition concerning the King;
My tongue is the pen of a ready writer. (Ps 45:1)

Let the words of my mouth and the meditation of
my heart be acceptable in Your sight, O Lord, my
strength and my Redeemer. (Ps 19:14)

My desire is to share what God has so graciously shared with me. May you personally experience the fullness of God in the testimonies of Jesus and all that is written on these pages. God is no respecter of persons. What He has done for so many, He will do for you. Come boldly to the throne of grace and ask Jesus. Today is your day of salvation. Encounter Jesus, His love and healing. Embark on a breathtaking adventure with God our Father!

You will show me the path of life;
In Your presence is fullness of joy;
At your right hand are pleasures forevermore. (Ps 16:11)

one

Broken Hearts

The Spirit of the Lord God is upon Me,
Because the Lord has anointed Me
To preach good tidings to the poor;
He has sent Me to heal the brokenhearted,
To proclaim liberty to the captives,
And the opening of the prison to those
who are bound; To proclaim the acceptable year
of the Lord, And the day of vengeance of our God;
To comfort all who mourn,
Is 61:1–2

Who are the brokenhearted? They are people crying out because life experiences wounded and crippled them. They are people you work with or sit next to in church. "They" may even be you.

In this fallen world, sin and suffering are realities. "From Adam's day to ours, tears have been shed, and a wail has been going up to heaven from the brokenhearted."[1]

Jesus came to give us life and life more abundantly. Are you experiencing abundant life and freedom? Jesus has given you exceedingly great and precious promises. He is ready, willing, and more than able to fulfill His promises to you today. Jesus wants to heal your broken heart.

Does your heart need healing? Do you experience one or more of the following?

> A pattern of recurring problems?
> Memories and thoughts that repeatedly bother you?
> Frequently feeling numb, overwhelmed, or sad?
> Feelings of shame, failure, and unworthiness?
> Avoidance of social situations and people?
> Unexpected outbursts of fear and/or anger?
> Addictive behavior?
> Difficulty in experiencing God, who is love?
> Emotional pain and absence of joy and peace?
> Loss or rejection you just can't "shake"?
> Trauma, such as abandonment, abuse, accidents, divorce, rape, death, war, disease?
> Being in an environment in which you suffer from the backlash of the above?
> Pain of watching someone suffer?

"God is near to those who have a broken heart and saves such as are crushed in spirit" (Ps 34:18 footnote SFLB). He is already present, closely watching. He attentively waits for the smallest invitation to be opened for Him to love the distressed. God has heard the cry coming from the brokenhearted, and He sent Jesus to heal broken hearts.

The devil, on the other hand, comes to break your heart by killing, stealing, and destroying. There is no reason to feel weak or ashamed because you need healing. You don't have to gut it out in your own strength. Jesus is healing millions of people today from the inside out. He loves to heal the brokenhearted. He invites you to come to Him for healing. Times of difficulty come into our lives, but oh what a change we experience when we receive the healing Jesus has for us. If your life is regularly comprised of more pain and anxiety than joy, consider that you may have a broken heart.

Many are ensnared in behavior and addictions out of sheer desperation, trying secretly to grasp a few moments of relief. No one is exempt, whether he or she is inside or outside the church. Multitudes are dying spiritually, mentally, and physically. Broken hearts can depress, break down physical bodies, and literally take lives. **The good news is** that no one has to remain miserable. Jesus has a better plan!

Floor Time For Me

In the past I experienced relentlessly stressful life situations and was suffering with severe back pain and related physical problems. Eventually I had back surgery and was confined to my bed for a month. After the bed rest, I attempted physically to strengthen my back, but I continued to experience pain.

During this same period of time, I was invited to minister with a team at the Toronto Airport Christian Fellowship. I probably would never have gone to Toronto had I not been desperate for God. After one of the morning sessions, I was overwhelmed and laid out on the floor by God's presence. Dr. Jesus had heart surgery planned for me that morning. As I lay on the floor, God brought to the surface memory after vivid memory concerning highly stressful situations I had experienced. For more than an hour, I alternately laughed with the joy of the Lord and cried as God removed my pain and healed me from my experiences that had literally crippled me. God did this through His love and power.

One meaning of "brokenhearted" in Greek is a heart completely crushed or shattered in pieces, but King Jesus is the

Healer who puts even Humpty Dumpty back together again.[2] "God, my God, I yelled for help and you put me together. God, you pulled me out of the grave, gave me another chance at life when I was down and out" (Ps 30:2–3, The Message). After this encounter with Jesus, my mind was cleared, my back was healed, and my health was restored. Jesus reached out and did what I could never have done for myself. He brought me back to abundant life.

The Whole Person

God's healing is as good for the body as it is for the soul and spirit. It is good whether it happens inside or out, outside or in, or any combination. Why do I use the term "healing the brokenhearted"? Because not only is it used in both the Old and New Testaments (Is 61:1 and Lk 4:18), but it is so important to God that He listed it as one of the specific items in Jesus's mission statement!

The Greek word for "heal" used in Luke 4:18 is "iaomai," which means to cure, heal and make whole.[3] To be cured or healed is certainly good and speaks of the absence of disease and restoration of function. In addition, wholeness means total complete healing of the entire person. Wholeness not only implies the absence of disease and restoration of function, but also includes the fullness of the benefits and blessings of God established in a person. A physician can diagnose and treat a condition. Jesus goes beyond curing and healing, He commands disease and evil to go and imparts wholeness to every aspect of the person.

Therefore, healing the brokenhearted describes complete healing salvation as the entire person is healed and transformed. It points toward addressing root causes of sin, sickness, and disease and being filled with the very goodness and love of God.

May His mission statement be found as a healing testimony in our lives and a passion in our hearts.

One of Paul's prayers is "May God himself, the God who makes everything holy and whole, put you together–spirit, soul, and body–and keep you fit for the coming of our Master, Jesus Christ. If he said it, he'll do it!" (1 Th 5:23–24, The Message). God knew you before conception and knit you together in the womb. He made you and therefore completely understands the function and interaction of your body, soul, and spirit. God's healing in one part of your body, soul, or spirit often results in healing your other parts. God demonstrates His nature and expresses His love no matter what part of the person He heals. His healing is contagious in that it spreads throughout the whole person. Addressing the things that God reveals to you prospers your body, soul, and spirit. Conversely, denying what He desires to do in you and refusing to cooperate with Him affects every aspect of your person (Ps 32:1–4).

Jesus asked which was easier, to forgive sin or to heal. The answer was and is resident in Him who asked the question! The answer is yes to both. *Both* are easy. Jesus's blood and His broken body can heal anything. Why make healing difficult when Jesus has already accomplished complete redemption for the whole person?

While ministering with my wife in Tanzania, Africa, a young woman came to Shereen for prayer. The young woman asked for prayer for a job. Because the music was so loud, my wife attempted to interview her further by speaking close to her right ear. The young woman immediately informed Shereen that she was deaf in her right ear. She further explained that she was twenty-three years old and had been sent by her parents to an expensive school to learn bookkeeping. The main reason this particular school was chosen was the job placement services provided upon completion of the program. After graduating, the young woman went to her job placement but was refused employment by the officer manager. The dejected young woman returned to the school and explained the situation. The school administrator explained that all the placements had been given away and her only choice was to return to the same business and make another attempt. She returned, but she was told to leave the premises and never return. The young woman believed the job that should have been hers was given to someone else. This young woman was desperate for a job. Her parents had invested all of their savings into her schooling so that she in turn would support the family with her wages as a bookkeeper. While she described the injustice that had occurred, my wife felt the Lord wanted to heal her right ear.

As Shereen asked her questions about her ear, the young woman answered politely; however, each answer was followed with "I really don't care about my ear; I need a job!" Eventually Shereen discovered that five years prior, in anger, the woman's brother had struck her on the side of her head because she had eaten his portion of the food their mother had left for them. She was knocked unconscious, and when she awoke in the hospital three days later, "All that was wrong with me was that I was deaf in my right ear." Shereen asked if she had forgiven her brother. She responded that of course she had; she was a Christian. Shereen was prompted by the Holy Spirit to ask again if she had forgiven her brother, and this time the young woman broke down and wept.

Right there and without further prompting, she forgave and released her brother for how he responded in anger toward her. Immediately, her right ear made a "pop" sound and opened up! The young woman started screaming, exclaiming that she could hear out of her right ear. She kept asking those around her to test it out "just to make sure." The young woman's right ear was healed, and with joy (and without prayer for her job situation) she left the church to tell her family what had occurred. Shereen and I soon left that church to travel to the next scheduled ministry venue.

Later we found out that the young woman testified at her church the following week. She returned to the business that had denied her employment. Instead of being confronted with the office manager who had rejected her the past two times, she was greeted by the owner. She discovered that the office manager had been fired the day prior. Not only was the young woman hired, but she was also given the office manager's position instead of the bookkeeper's position! This young woman was healed spiritually, emotionally, and physically, and God opened the door for her to support her family with new employment.

Living Water

One aspect of healing is cleansing. In John chapter 13, Jesus shared a valuable truth with the disciples by washing their feet. As Jesus approached Peter, he objected and declared that Jesus would never wash his feet. I believe the reason Peter made this declaration was because he was focused on only a single aspect of Jesus's identity. Peter was looking at the gesture as simply an act of service and couldn't imagine his King humbling Himself to serve him in such a menial way. Jesus's intention was much greater, He desired to teach the disciples by word and deed. Jesus replied that if Peter did not allow Him to wash his feet, Peter would not belong to Him. Peter answered that he wanted as much of Jesus as he could get; he asked for his hands and head to be washed also!

When we belong to Christ, we desire deep in our hearts for Him to thoroughly wash us; including our feet. Our feet represent our walk in this world, and Jesus wants to wash the world off of us. He continues to be our example, and His washing is far greater than what we can do for ourselves. It is good to ask for all the washing we can get—foot washing, cleansing the soul, and baptism.

Holy Fire

John the Baptist prophesied that Jesus would baptize us with the Holy Spirit and fire. There are various functions of holy fire, one of which is to burn up and destroy the works of the devil (Acts 10:38). His fire literally destroys pain and the effects of damaging experiences. His fire is more powerful and precise than the best laser used by doctors. His fire can and does easily remove pain, and then He skillfully puts the puzzle pieces of our lives back together again. And the result is something brand new!

The touch of His hand, a glance of His eye, a loving smile—any way He imparts His perfect love can bring radical kingdom transformation. How do we experience this fire? We simply ask Jesus to baptize us in His fire. His fire burns off whatever binds us and sets us free. The fire of God also ignites His passion in our hearts. When the fire gets hot, ask Jesus, "More fire! Don't stop!"

Prayer

Jesus, You love me beyond measure. You passionately desire to fix me up and put me back together again. Come with Your love and Your healing power and make me completely whole. Amen.

two

The Wonderful Cross

*who Himself bore our sins in His own body on the
tree, that we, having died to sins, might live for
righteousness–by whose stripes you were healed.*
1 Pet 2:24

The cross is where we begin; it points to how we live in Jesus.
Jesus openly revealed God's love for us when He chose death
and the agony of the cross in exchange for a relationship with
us. He did what He did because we are His joy. He paid the
price for my sin and yours, as well as the sin of humankind for
all time. Life comes out of His death.

Jesus's sacrifice of taking our place and penalty is the
ultimate demonstration of God's love for all. The heart of
God is in the cross of Christ. It will take all eternity to grasp
all of God's great love that He demonstrated on the cross.
Our bliss is overwhelming as we receive more and more of
His goodness and His perfect love, which increasingly fill and
enfold us. The following is one of my favorite hymns—majestic
when sung to music and beautiful as a written expression of
the love of God.

The Love of God (stanza three)
Could we with ink the ocean fill,
And were the skies of parchment made,
Were every stalk on earth a quill,
And every man a scribe by trade;
To write the love of God above
Would drain the ocean dry;
Nor could the scroll contain the whole,
Though stretched from sky to sky.[1]

The Ministry of Exchange

Simply put, sin separates us from having a relationship with God. What Jesus did on the cross restores our relationship back to God. The word "reconciled" or "reconciliation" here means to exchange, make right, or restore.[2] Here are a few truths written in the Bible about reconciliation:

"For if when we were enemies we were reconciled to God through the death of His Son, much more, having been reconciled, we shall be saved by His life." (Rom 5:10)

"and by Him to reconcile all things to Himself, whether things on earth or things in heaven, having made peace through the blood of His cross." (Col 1:20)

"Now all things are of God, who has reconciled us to Himself through Jesus Christ, and given us the ministry of reconciliation," (2 Cor 5:18)

Exchange is a radical act when we consider that Jesus takes all of our garbage while we receive all of His goodness. Jesus restored our relationship with God and healed us completely.

The cross is a finished work, past tense; it has already been accomplished. It is not earned. It is "done," not "do." How awesomely amazing that Jesus exchanged His life so we can have new life in Him. He is our substitute. The transaction is completed when we receive Jesus and all He accomplished. Then we become recipients of all the benefits Christ purchased at the cross.

God does more than just tear negative things off people. "O taste and see that the Lord is good;" (Ps 34:8a) is an open invitation to come and experience the goodness of God as well. What did Jesus die on the cross for if it were not to purchase this exchange for everyone? This *wonderful* exchange was purchased for you by Jesus at the cross:

- All the blessings of God in Christ instead of the curse of the law
- Life and life more abundantly instead of sin and death
- Identity as a son of God instead of identity as a servant
- Friendship with God instead of estrangement
- Good news instead of hopelessness
- Praise instead of depression
- Gladness instead of sadness
- Healing instead of brokenness, sickness, and pain
- Liberty instead of captivity
- Recovery of sight instead of blindness
- Future and hope instead of loss and disappointment
- Rest instead of heavy burdens
- Peace instead of chaos
- Comfort and rejoicing instead of tears
- Righteousness instead of unrighteousness
- Fullness instead of emptiness
- Cleansing blood instead of guilt
- Healing stripes instead of disease
- Justice instead of injustice

- Right instead of wrong
- Redemption instead of punishment
- Opening prison doors instead of being bound
- Joy and dancing instead of mourning
- Beauty instead of ashes
- The Spirit of adoption instead of spirit of bondage to fear
- Double honor instead of shame
- A heart of flesh instead of a heart of stone
- Good plans instead of evil plans
- Restoration of years instead of lost time
- Love instead of hatred
- Divine nature instead of godlessness
- Prosperity instead of poverty
- Unmerited favor instead of failure
- Grace and truth instead of the law
- Rooted and grounded in love instead of instability
- Reconciliation with God instead of alienation
- Love, power, and a sound mind instead of fear
- The light of the glorious gospel instead of spiritual blindness
- Forgiveness instead of sin
- Being found in Christ instead of being lost
- Holiness instead of wickedness
- Strength instead of weakness
- Wholeness instead of brokenness
- Mercy instead of judgment
- Eternal life instead of hell
- Fullness instead of emptiness
- Victory instead of defeat
- Blessings instead of curses
- The Light of the world instead of darkness
- The Kingdom of Heaven instead of this present world

The spotless Lamb of God, the King of Glory, was treated with contempt. The One who *is* love was an outcast, despised and rejected. Psalm 69:4 prophetically states that He was hated without a cause. The ultimate demonstration of love was that Jesus, the perfectly innocent God-man, "took the rap" and paid the full penalty for all our sin. Jesus, full of grace and truth, was judged for our sins and transgressions. Grasping what Jesus did for us on that wonderful cross reveals God's love and the value He places upon us. He demonstrated infinite kindness in the exchange. Christ died for you. *You* are the joy that was set before Him! Jesus was thinking of you, and this enabled Him to endure the suffering He experienced.

Forgiveness and Healing in the Cross

The footnote and center note of the Spirit-Filled Life Bible for Isaiah 53:4–6 state the following:

4a: Jesus took upon Himself our sicknesses and diseases
4b: He carried away the burden of our grief, sorrow, and pain
5a: Jesus was pierced for our rebellion and trespasses
5b: He was crushed for our tendency to sin
5c: He was punished so that we could have complete peace (shalom)
5d: And by His stripes we are healed (made whole)
6c: The punishment for the sin of the entire human race was placed on Jesus

What I love about each of these verses above is that they are applied to the physical body, the soul, and the spirit of a person. Therefore, Jesus was pierced and crushed for our sin, our mental anguish, *and* our diseases. And the best part is that Jesus shares His healing and forgiveness not just with one person but with whoever comes to Him. He asks us to place and, yes, even push our sin, disease, and pain into His stripes. Can you ask Jesus for more of His finished work and the exchange He accomplished for you at the cross?

Prayer

Wonderful Jesus, thank you for the wonderful cross and the love You displayed there for me. Help me fully exchange my life for the abundant life You purchased at Calvary. Thank you for forgiving my sin, healing my disease, carrying away my pain, and giving me Your peace. Heal me at the deepest level—body, soul, and spirit. I love You, Jesus. Amen.

three

The Love of God

Jesus Christ is the same yesterday,
today, and forever.
Heb 13:8

Agape, perfect love of God, is used throughout this book, although it is most often referred to simply as "love." His extravagant love is identical today to the love He had when He chose to give His life on the cross two thousand years ago.

One summer I ministered with a short-term mission team at a church in Londrina, Brazil. A young woman came to the church with her sister. She used to attend the church before she became involved with drugs. When she walked in, the church pastor immediately hugged her, and the young woman dropped to the floor on her knees. The ladies of the church kissed, hugged, and loved her. She wept until tissues all over the floor surrounded her. I could hear the hearts of the church members: "We were so concerned about you. We missed you so much. We were incomplete without you. Thank God you are home. Welcome back to the house of the Lord. We love you." A woman from the church helped her up from the floor, sat her in a chair, and washed her feet. At this point the young woman's sister, who had brought her back to church, began to dance before the Lord. A few minutes later, the young woman put on sackcloth and again knelt on the floor. Soon after, the sister helped the young woman take off her sackcloth, and they both danced before the Lord together. We experienced heaven on earth as worship reached a crescendo. The whole church came forward, and we all celebrated with the angels. A living parable of God's extravagant love was openly displayed that night. The beauty and love of God's restoration was humbling and awe inspiring. God's love is kind and His kindness draws us to repentance (1 Cor 13:4 and Rom 2:4).

The Gift of Grace

There may seem to be innumerable reasons why someone does not "deserve" grace, the agape love of God. Then we remember that apart from Christ, no one is worthy and none of us deserve His grace. A person cannot earn healing; a person cannot earn the grace that has already been given to him or her. Someone may be in an embarrassing, hopeless situation and wallowing in a pit. Our first response might be an automatic solution of "you ought to…" or "change your behavior," or "you got what you deserve." Yet, would you be shocked to hear Jesus say, "Don't advise him or her to read the Bible more, pray more, or do more in the church"?

My friends, Mike and Beverley Robinson, shared a testimony about a strip-tease club owner who had become a Christian and started attending a local church. At the next church members' meeting, the pastor of the church told his congregation that no one was to tell the strip-tease club owner that how he earned his living was not in keeping with being a Christian. This was the job of the Holy Spirit, who alone could convict him. The pastor encouraged the congregation to extend the same grace to the club owner that God had extended to them. The people of the congregation did as they were told and, with baited breath, waited every Sunday for the business owner to make his confession. Then one Sunday the man asked the pastor if he could share a testimony. The pastor agreed, and when it was time to share, the man stood up and said, "I have been coming to this church for a while now and have really felt loved. I just wanted to let everyone here know that the Holy Spirit has convicted me of my wrongdoing, and from now on I will no longer water down anybody's drink when he or she comes into my club." He then smiled and sat down! It obviously became a learning experience for the whole church. Long story short, after several more weeks, he again gave his testimony—this time to say he had sold his club and was going into full-time ministry for Jesus. He became an evangelist. We all need God's love and grace.

Love's Offer

Love is the essential key to a relationship with God and others. The two great commandments are to love God and love others (Mt 22:36–40). God enables us to love Him and to love others by first receiving His love for ourselves. God's love fills us and fulfills His will for us.

Jesus's love for the woman caught in adultery was expressed by first eliminating her accusers and then drawing her attention to a fresh reality by asking the question, "Who accuses you now?" She received His love gift and then answered, "No one, Lord." Jesus replied, "Neither do I condemn you." Then He called her to wholeness, a brand-new way of life, saying, "Go and sin no more" (Jn 7:53–8:12). If she had depended on her self-worth to receive God's gift of love, she would have disqualified herself and never been able to accept His love offer. The offer of love is not dependent on our own personal merit.

Receive the Offer

An account that illustrates how much we are loved is in John chapter 11. Jesus's friend Lazarus had died four days prior, and when Jesus finally arrived at Lazarus's tomb, he wept. Jesus then commanded the stone to be removed from the tomb. Once the stone was rolled away, Jesus commanded Lazarus to "come forth." Then He told the people watching to loose and unwrap Lazarus. God never intended us, the objects of His love, to label ourselves as dead and hopeless problems. God's love for you is stronger than any experience or problem you face. He will roll away your stone and loose and unwrap you. His love for you is stronger than death.

Without the love of God, you are not truly alive. The good news is that love is a choice made possible by receiving what has already been given to you by God. Therefore, "love me" is not a selfish prayer; instead it opens the door to receive the love He is poised to pour out. Living out of love is to live life out of His life and fullness. Put another way, abundant life is living in Jesus's love and life. Love transforms more deeply than anything else because love never fails. "Fill me with Your love" is a scriptural prayer. Father God wants you to experience and be filled with His love (Eph 3:17–19). He desires that you be filled and fulfilled with His perfect love and His abundant life, now and forever.

Now that your love tanks are filled, you can minister the love and life of Jesus to each person you encounter. When you pour out to others and your tanks begin to empty, ask Him to fill your love tanks up again and top you off to overflowing!

A More Excellent Way

True excellence is not produced by trying harder in our own strength or asking God to bless our personal plans. We do not benefit from performing even the most awesome works for God if love is lacking. God's love is the more excellent way that is necessary, especially when exercising the gifts of the Holy Spirit. If love is not present, the essential nature of God is not present.

Love profits all and results in the deepest healing. Throughout the time I have ministered healing to broken hearts, I have seen that encountering Jesus and His love can accomplish in minutes what counseling alone has taken years to do. This statement does not mean I am against counseling; I have a master's degree in counseling. However, what I have learned from my experiences is that Jesus's love is a more excellent way.

We love God because He first loved us. The Father Himself loves you so much that He sent Jesus. God's desire is for each person to enjoy and relate to Him in love. The Holy Spirit, Who has been given to you, has poured the love of God into your heart. The same Holy Spirit God sent us cries out: Papa, Father, witnessing that we are children of God and heirs (Rom 8:12-17). You are no longer a slave, but a son/daughter with a full inheritance of God through Jesus. You are related by blood (the blood of Jesus), and you belong to God and His family. The fact is that God loves you like He loves His own Son, Jesus! He wants the love, with which He loves Jesus, to be in you and every member of His body (Jn 17:20-26). You have access to intimacy with the perfect Father with perfect love.

God's purpose is for His sons and daughters to first receive and then minister in "the love anointing." Through scripture we know that faith works through love, and love invites the presence and power of God. Look at all that is possible through love: patience in suffering, tenderness toward others, contentment, focus on God instead of on self, treating others with honor, ruling out retaliation, forgetting offense, selecting mercy instead of judgment, rejoicing in the triumph of good, believing the best of others, pointing others to Jesus rather than dismissing them, and persevering in adversity (1 Cor 13:1–7). Each time we call to mind His patient love in our lives, we are empowered to express His patient love to others. How important is love? Let all that you do be done with love (1 Cor 16:14).

Love Is Greater

Love remains long after God removes the details of past pain. I think the most amazing part about the whole childbirth process is, as numerous mothers have told me, how quickly the mother forgets the pain of childbirth. Instead, what they *can* remember is the love and joy they experienced while holding their newborn. Love is remembered more than the details of the birth pains! Likewise, God offers us His love to replace pain we have experienced. God's love is greater than sin, sickness, pain, and death.

The following testimony was written by Launi who describes an encounter she had with Jesus:

I experienced a life-changing encounter with Jesus like never before. I have encountered Jesus and received my fair share of deliverance and healing, but this was beyond anything else. The revelation I received and the gift of life I got on this day were just too enormous to compare with any other.

It began as a training class on prayer for healing the brokenhearted. I was invited by my pastor and his wife to accompany them to a seminar at the Healing Rooms in Santa Maria, California. I was happy to join them and so excited because my passion and heart is to pray for healing of the brokenhearted.

After the teaching, Stuart decided we should practice on each other. In my mind I was thinking it was a great idea, I wanted to start praying over people! As we began to pray, the Lord told me, "Get prayer for your stomach." I had been suffering from ulcer pain on and off for many years and was taking pain medication. I began to argue with God a little; I wanted to be the one praying. I didn't want to *receive* prayer. As I was having this conversation with God, Stuart had a word of knowledge about someone with stomach pain and pointed to his own stomach as a reference. It was the exact same place where I had pain! I knew at that point God had won the argument. I was getting in the hot seat that day.

Prayer began by asking Jesus when these ulcers started. When I asked Jesus this, it was as if I was taken down a rabbit hole in time, and I began to see bits and pieces of my past. I thought maybe it was when I was doing a ton of drugs, but I just kept going farther. I thought maybe the stress from abusive relationships was it, but I kept moving back in time. Eventually, I stopped when I was seventeen years old; I was in a doctor's office. The doctor told me I had ulcers and that they would never go away. So I thought, "That's it! The doctor cursed me!" But as I began to share out loud what I was experiencing, Stuart suggested I ask Jesus to shine His light on that memory and show me more. So I did…and He did. I was suddenly taken a little farther back to another doctor's office. I was now in an abortion clinic. My heart sank into my feet and all that was left of me were sobs. I just sat crying for a while until Shereen asked me if I was able to share what was going on.

I began to share that Jesus helped me see it was an abortion. Then as soon as I spoke it, I could see myself on the second bed where I got the second abortion two years later. Again I melted into a sobbing mess. As I tried to share through my tears and groans of pain, I was able to see inside my stomach. I could see two holes in the lining, and immediately I knew that the holes were my two babies.

Still weeping and writhing in heartache, grief, and pain, I asked Jesus to come and love me. I found myself in a vast area full of white—nothing but white. It was just me standing there. It was then that I knew I had not fully forgiven myself and that I needed to speak those words. So I said it: "I forgive you, Launi." Right after that, I felt a presence with me. I looked up and it was Jesus! He was standing in front of me with two tiny babies—one in each arm, cradled more perfectly than I have ever seen one hold a baby. I looked at them in awe and slight fear, but I somehow knew it was perfect and good.

I began to think of the four children I had at home and how I had made mistakes and hurt them. I had always been able to go to them and tell them how sorry I was and ask their forgiveness for my mistakes. I was able to hold them in my arms and look them in the eyes and they always respond, "It's OK, Mommy." But with my two babies that I hurt the most, I could never say, "Mommy is so sorry. I made a mistake; please forgive me. I love you." I wept more intensely than I ever had. Soon after, I remembered that Jesus brought my children to me in the Spirit and this was my chance to tell them how sorry I was. However, before I could speak, they spoke to me through their eyes. It's really impossible to put in human words. Their voices didn't come out of their mouths. It was as if they spoke with their eyes. It was the most *amazing* thing! "It's OK, Mommy. We've always forgiven you." *That was it!* I was undone! I thought I would simply turn inside out at that point. Soon after, I saw Jesus wrap His white robe around them. They were now hidden from my sight as He gently walked them to another place. I just watched in awe. Jesus then turned to me and told me that it was OK to say good-bye; I would see them again. So I let them go.

After I saw Jesus and my children were gone, I was filled with joy and peace. I felt so alive and free I could hardly contain myself. As this happened, I also had a physical sensation like warm milk being poured down my throat and going into my stomach. I could feel a coating and a filling like nothing I had ever felt in my life. As I turned my attention toward what was happening in my body, I realized I had no pain in my stomach *at all!* All the burning was gone, and all I could feel was peace and comfort. My stomach felt so soft and whole. Jesus healed me!

God performed open-heart surgery on me that day, and I didn't even see it coming. My life was changed forever. It's like I see things with new eyes. I have not had problems with my stomach since then, and I no longer take the pain medication. When I think of my children who are with Him, I no longer hurt. I rejoice! I never thought I could be *this* healed. Praise God!

Healing Love

Only God's love and presence can fill, heal, and bring a person to true health and wholeness. To know God is to know love because God *is* love. Receiving God's love changes and strengthens us profoundly. His power works within us and His love is provision for our journey. Love is the master key of the Kingdom that opens hearts, heals, and transforms.

1 Peter 4:8 states that love will *cover* a multitude of sins. Peter is encouraging us to have fervent love for each other because in doing so we will spend time seeing the good (treasure) instead of pointing out the sin in each other. Having love for each

other is wonderful, but the love God has for us does not simply cover sin. God's love *overwhelms* sin. In other words, God's great love overpowers, overcomes, devastates, and crushes sin. God's love covers not *just* a multitude of sin, but *all* sin, sickness, and disease! Jesus's act of love was laying down His life for us and then enabling us to be filled with His love, power, and authority to overcome evil and live victoriously (Col 2:13–15).

God wants us to *experience* this love. We are able to experience His love even though our human minds cannot fully grasp it. This love transforms our whole being and opens the door for us to be filled full of God. This love steps into all things possible.

Love is not optional. I have observed the problems that occur in relationships and organizations when love was considered optional. Common goals enable people to agree and walk together in unity, but God's love is the perfect *bond* of unity (Col 3:14). When love grows cold, the presence and power of God diminish. Without God's love present and practiced, deterioration and decline occur.

Fear and Defensiveness

Could God's love be less than perfect when He is perfect and He is love? God's perfect love is the antidote for many things. Have you ever seen a baby wrapped up for a chilly day by a new parent? The baby is dressed in a onesie, long-sleeved shirt, sweatshirt, wool sweater, heavy jeans, two pairs of socks, boots, insulated hooded jacket, wool beanie, and mittens! This baby cannot even move his or her arms and legs—there are more clothes than baby!

Likewise, over-defensiveness becomes such a burden that it binds us up and then fear steals our freedom. God's perfect love breaks down our walls of defensiveness and casts out all fear (1

Jn 4:18). Perfect love allows a person to experience a safe place in God. God's perfect love frees the heart to open further and receive peace and trust in Him. God's perfect love continues to fill us with His presence, healing, life, and even more love. You were made for this wonderful, unending, unfailing love. The God-shaped hole in your heart can only be filled by God and His perfect love. Even the best parents and best friends cannot meet the need that cries from the heart. God's complete, perfect love has nothing lacking or missing. This flawless, unlimited love consummates you—you are complete in Him (Col 2:10).

Ask God to touch your heart with His love. Now open your heart wide to Him and allow Him to fill you to overflowing with His love. You can trust Him and rest in His love for you.

Love Lifted Me

refrain
Love lifted me!
Love lifted me!
When nothing else could help,
Love lifted me![1]

Expressing Love

God's promise to Abraham and to you in Christ is that He will bless you and make you a blessing (Gen 12:2, Gal 3:13–14). Blessing is not limited to a single prayer or a verbal formula. Expressing the goodness of God is more than just words; you are created and designed to *be* a blessing (1 Pet 3:8–9). Speaking life and blessing expresses the love of God. Your words have the power of life and death (Pr 18:21). You can impart life through what you say and you can impart death with that very same tongue. You bless in a very tangible way with what you say.

However, it's not just the words you utter; it's what you carry inside you that makes you a blessing. When you receive and give God's love, you bring the blessings of heaven to earth.

Blessing is an expression of God's love that also displaces a critical spirit. Have you ever met someone who is critical? I worked with a person who was relentlessly critical about *everything*. It seemed as if he spent his all of his time evaluating and looking for things to criticize. I decided to begin speaking to him and being a blessing every time I encountered him. Guess what happened next? I became a blessing to this person! Over a period of time he began to receive substantial healing.

While on a ministry trip in Germany, my wife and I walked briskly down a platform to catch a train to downtown Dusseldorf. A young man sitting on a bench eyed me with scorn and spit on the ground. He then stood up and yelled at me in German. A friend promptly interpreted what he said: "You don't care about anything or anybody except getting where you want to go." I stopped, turned toward the young man, stretched out my hand, and said, "I bless you with God's love in the name of Jesus." He looked at me for a few moments and then quietly sat down. It is hard to continue in anger when you've just received God's blessing!

Prayer

Father God, fill me with Your great love again and again. I open my heart to You. Love me in the deepest part of my heart. Father, wrap Your arms of love around me. Rest Your presence in and upon me. Jesus, fill me with Your great love. I want purity and simplicity of devotion to You, free from anxiety and full of joy. Holy Spirit of God, fill me continually. Give me the grace to enjoy Your love daily. Overflow Your love in me and funnel it through me. Amen.

four

Tell Jesus

Search me, O God, and know my heart, try me and know my anxieties; And see if there is any wicked way in me, And lead me in the way everlasting.
Ps 139:23–24

I think we can all agree that we are in a race, but according to Hebrews 12:1, it is impossible to run the race while carrying baggage filled with heavy burdens. Attempting to bury our "stuff" and prevent it from being exposed actually steals life from us. Taking time to honestly share our feelings with God is essential for an intimate relationship with Him, as well as for physical, mental, and emotional well-being. While I was attending an ordination class, one of the pastors concisely stated, "If you ain't who you is, you is who you ain't." There is great value in his statement because I believe it summarizes the importance of being honest with God and ourselves. If we practice anything other than being honest with God, we end up acting like someone whom we really aren't!

Being honest with God is made easy by knowing the love God has for us. This type of honesty actually honors Him. We may think, "If He really knew everything about me, He wouldn't love me anymore." Yet, beloved, He *does* know it all, and He loves us. Talk about grace, mercy, and blessing!

David asked God to know his heart and to surface his anxiety and any wickedness. Anxiety may not initially be willful sin, but it is sin nonetheless. Christ, our Burden-Bearer, did not die so we could carry heavy burdens. Carrying burdens is as productive as attempting to accelerate to maximum speed in a vehicle with the parking brake fully engaged. When we sincerely express and confess to God, He shows us our worries, sins, and the way home to Him.

Pour out your complaint before God. David did and he received divine results! When David was under fire, he honestly recognized and expressed his feelings. This enabled him to turn his focus on God and His goodness. You belong to Him and He is your refuge, so pour out your heart before Him.

True peace does not exist apart from truth in communication. If we are not honest with God, we cannot be honest with anyone else. You may be saying at this point, "Stuart, why are you stating the obvious? This is such a simple concept." Yes, I agree completely. It *is* simple, and when you actually do it, it brings peace.

Forgive

The only way we can completely forgive others is first to personally receive God's forgiveness. If we confess our sins, God is faithful to forgive and cleanse us from *all* unrighteousness (I Jn 1:9). Consider all you have done and all that God has forgiven you. From this vantage point, extending forgiveness to others takes on a richer meaning. Allow the double-edged sword of the Spirit to work in your life by extending the forgiveness you yourself have already received.

Forgiving is necessary to continue a relationship, whether with God or with others. God calls us to forgive both the offender and the sin. As we read in the Lord's Prayer, Jesus instructed us that we would be forgiven to the same degree that we forgive others (Mt 6:12). His love empowers us to go beyond just choosing to forgive but to extend deep forgiveness from the heart.

Granting deep forgiveness from the heart is not contingent upon a change of attitude or behavior from a person who has sinned against us. There are actually no prerequisites to forgiving. Why is forgiveness so important to Jesus? Because Jesus paid for forgiveness with His very blood. To refuse to forgive is to withhold from others the forgiveness He purchased for *all* at Calvary. He tells us to do what He did. He tells us to forgive. Jesus described the Kingdom of Heaven concerning forgiveness in Matthew 18:21–35. The last verses state that our Father God will deliver us to the torturers if we do not forgive others and their trespasses from our hearts. These may sound like harsh words, but in reality, refusing to forgive opens us up to sickness, torment within, and conflict with everyone around us. There are negative consequences if we choose to disobey God, which are vividly described in these verses. Even though Jesus commanded us to forgive from the heart, He never said we couldn't ask Him to help us do it! Forgiveness frees us as well as the person we forgive because it cancels the debt owed to us. To forgive is an essential beginning (not the end) of healing. (Jesus Himself is the beginning and end of healing.) And since God's love does not keep an account of wrongs, neither should ours. Cut someone loose from the debt they owe you and by doing so you cut yourself loose as well.

The following testimony is from Carole, a precious friend whom I minister with at the Healing Rooms of the Santa Maria Valley.

The Wisconsin Testimony

My husband, Rudy, our son, and I were living in North Carolina when Rudy's dad asked if we could come and help him run his farm in Wisconsin. Rudy's brother had been running the farm but had to leave because he had gotten sick from mold poisoning in his lungs caused by the silage used to feed cattle in the winter months. We accepted his offer, and we packed up and moved to Wisconsin.

Everything went fine until one day a government agent came to the farm and offered to pay Rudy *not* to plant hay. Rudy took the offer, but when his dad found out, he was angry and started bad-mouthing us to the neighbors. I was nine months pregnant at the time, and my mother and niece had come to be with me when I had the baby.

One day, while Rudy was out in the field, the sheriff came to the door and presented me with eviction papers from Rudy's dad! We left immediately and visited with Rudy's brother nearby until our baby was born. Shortly afterward we moved to California, where Rudy had been offered a job.

We were pretty hurt and devastated by the eviction, which came during a time of major transitions. We didn't even know how to forgive Rudy's dad. Actually, we thought Rudy's dad should apologize to us and ask our forgiveness, which he never did. When we surrendered to God, we heard teaching on forgiveness, and we decided to forgive. We were not aware, however, that we had not completely forgiven.

Decades later, in February of 2013, Rudy's nephew and wife came to visit me. We had a wonderful time together and, one night after dinner, Rudy's nephew asked me what happened to cause us to leave the farm in Wisconsin. I told him about being evicted from the farm and being left out of Rudy's dad's will. He shared with me that Rudy's dad had a difficult childhood because his older siblings picked on him mercilessly while growing up, and his mom didn't hear or see a lot of it. I found out that Rudy's dad's most cherished childhood memory was following his dad around the farm, away from the torment of his siblings.

As we continued to talk, Rudy's nephew shared that Rudy's mother had had twins weighing twelve pounds each, and the doctor had to cut them out of her! Her last pregnancy was with Rudy, which finished her off. She was never again able to be a wife to her husband. Because of this, Rudy's dad blamed Rudy for losing his wife. I was able to see Rudy's dad hurt for the first time and from his point of view. I cried because of his frustration and disappointment.

I have come to realize that there are layers of forgiveness, and I needed to forgive that last "layer." I immediately shredded the will, eviction papers, and some letters I had saved and removed everything from my house pertaining to the time we spent in Wisconsin. I washed Rudy's dad and myself in the blood of Jesus, and now truly am free from anything left unforgiven toward Rudy's dad. God is beyond good—He is awesome!

More about Forgiveness

Restore a relationship if it can be restored. As much as is possible, be at peace with all people is a scripture I live my life by (Rom 12:18). Forgiveness prepares the way for a relationship to be restored, but at the same time I believe you cannot make restoration happen. Even God does not *force* restoration with everyone, although Jesus purchased redemption for *all* at the cross. You can be filled with the love of God and desire the best for all people. After you forgive him or her, place the person in Jesus's hands and leave him or her there. Jesus is more than able to take care of what you commit to Him.

Forgiving yourself is just as necessary as forgiving others. To forgive others but then selectively blame yourself is rejecting the forgiveness Jesus purchased at the cross for you. You do not belong to yourself; you have been bought with a price. You neither have the right to sin against yourself nor do you have the right to withhold forgiveness from yourself. You are saved by grace—continue in it. Agree with Jesus and cut yourself a grace break. The Bible declares in Romans 8:31, if God is for you, who can be against you? This can also be applied to yourself. As you consider the personal impact of this statement, do you really want to be against yourself? Of course not! My suggestion is for you to practice and establish the habit of regularly forgiving yourself.

Taking communion is one way God has provided for us to remember Jesus and then receive and extend His forgiveness to others. In this respect, think of taking communion as the reset button on the electronics of your heart and mind. Free yourself and free others.

Washing and Cleansing

We need washing and cleansing from the things done to us as well as the things we do. Some hurt is intentional, some unintentional, and some only perceived, but we need to be washed and cleansed from it all. The solution is not in playing the "blame game." Living in this world sometimes includes walking through deep weeds and stepping in a large pile of poop. The animal did not set a premeditated trap, yet it left undeniable evidence that smells and clings to shoes like bubble gum on a hot summer day. It is not my fault, not the animal's fault, or any person's deliberate action. Yet I am left with the challenging task of scrubbing my shoes and thoroughly washing my hands of the experience.

Just as bathing physically cleans, the water of the Word spiritually cleans. The effects of living in this world can be washed away. How can we proactively wash ourselves? Remember, we are the house of God; we are His holy dwelling place. Therefore, regular fellowship with God invites Him into His dwelling place, where we can regularly bathe in the river of God (His presence), which cleanses us. If we have something bothersome in our lives, we have the privilege to pray and stay in the cleansing presence of God until it is washed away.

In addition, being continually filled with the Holy Spirit washes and cleanses us as well. Jesus promised the Holy Spirit to those who believe in Him. Likewise, He spoke concerning the Holy Spirit that rivers of living water would flow out of our hearts. As God the Holy Spirit increasingly fills the heart, room for sin, unforgiveness, and unhealthy attachments diminish. Asking for and continually being filled with the Holy Spirit fills us with a fresh supply of pure, life-giving water.

God can do an infinitely deeper, more thorough cleansing in us than we can do ourselves. Asking and yielding to God is our part in the cleansing process, which allows Him to accelerate His work in one area after another in our lives. As we choose to humble ourselves before Him, He lifts us up. God desires to set us free from all our wrong thinking and to know Him more.

God of the Deep Things

It is possible to read, believe, and quote the Word of God without allowing God to apply it deeply to your heart. Agreement with God is more than a matter of words; it is yielding the heart. Likewise, out of the heart come the issues of life, which include our thought life, will, and emotions.

God wants to surface the feelings deep in your heart. To know deep healing is to experience God's presence in your depths. Asking God to search me and know my heart is to invite Him to "plumb my depths, get in my stuff, rock my world!" One radical prayer that brings results is "Do whatever it takes to set me free and heal me!"

Cooperating with God in this process requires obedience. Remember that God loves you with perfect love. If you feel pain, call to mind that He is the One healing you, and He has exactly what you need. He already carried away your pain at the cross and healed you (Is 53), and now He is giving you even more of what He already bought for you. When God pulls the roots, it may hurt momentarily, but He removes obstacles from your path so you can be free. As you share your deep feelings with God, He will put more grace deep within you. He considers sharing your feelings with Him part of an intimate relationship with Him. The fact is that you feel what you feel, true or false. As feelings surface and are expressed, the lies and false mindsets then become apparent in the presence of the Truth.

Jesus has given us the awesome privilege of relating to Him as a friend, not as a servant. True friendship includes both parties sharing from the heart. Jesus shares with us all the things the Father has shared with Him. Therefore there is no fear of sharing our weaknesses with Jesus when we know His love and our identity are in Him. To personalize this, true communication includes honest sharing with Him, not hiding your feelings from Him. If you want God to be real with you, be real with Him. Draw near to God, and He will draw near to you. God knows you completely, so why even try being someone else by attempting to hide things from God?

Repentance

Repentance is not attained by trying to be a better person—husband, wife, mother, father, employee, church member, etcetera. Repentance is to completely change the way we think with God's help. It is agreeing with God that sin is sin, and His ways and thoughts are perfect. This is a far cry from "there is a better way to do this."

To dance around what needs change without going to God is wasted effort. No matter the platitudes, the detailed plans, and even a small army to help, in-depth change and restoration will not happen. Why? Because if the root of the problem is in the heart and mind of the person, only God and His truth can address it. With repentance, doing things God's way is completely different than simply finding a better way of doing things. Plainly, you were made in the image of God; you are God's royal house, His dwelling place. A royal house is not a garbage dump. Regularly take out all your garbage to Jesus, and leave it with Him. Repentance leads to healing.

Change of Heart

The Christian life comes with a "subject to change" clause. Despite our feelings, *change* is part of following Jesus. The Holy Spirit escorts us to new situations and new locations. We can choose to be obedient and grateful, despite the stress that change can often bring, knowing deep within our hearts that God has the best plan for us. God's purpose for change is to diminish the distance between where we presently are to where we are seated with Christ in Heavenly places.

Attempting to change without approaching Jesus is putting the cart before the horse. God wants to help us change by transforming us and the way we think. In contrast, satan wants to label us as failures and immobilize us with the past and judgment. Jesus reminds us who and Whose we are. He is the door through Whom we leave the past behind and enter into new, abundant life.

Remain flexible in order to receive encouragement, wisdom, direction, and correction. Thank Him and agree with Him. All disciples of Jesus are learners who are changing and being changed. Once we understand this, we will gladly exhibit the fruit of change and transformation that advances the Kingdom.

Prayer

Thank You for the grace to share honestly with You. You know me better than I know myself. Search, change, transform, and set me free. Create a clean heart in me, renew a right spirit within me, and restore to me the joy of my salvation. I choose to walk in the spirit and love. As I go deep into You, go deep into me. Minister Your truth in my deepest part. Help me learn and grow in You. I love You, Jesus. Amen.

five

It's Not Always a Broken Heart

*Beloved, do not think it strange concerning
the fiery trial which is to try you, as though
some strange thing happened to you;*
1 Peter 4:12

Just because your heart hurts doesn't mean it is broken! Sometimes we get confused when we experience difficulties, but there is a difference between having a broken heart and going through difficulties. Although they both feel uncomfortable, they are quite different.

It would be unnecessary to address trials, troubles, and suffering if they were not real. They are very real and authentic Christian experiences that train, test, and prove us in preparation for promotion. Passing through trials with God strengthens our faith, trust, and relationship with Him. Denying the reality of trials ignores scripture and positions us for a "what did I do wrong?" mindset. The Bible would be drastically different if trials were deleted. In Hebrews chapter 11, the "hall of fame of faith" tells us about people whose promises were fulfilled through trials and the testing of their faith. A faith without difficulties would require preaching about a different Christ who was not tempted or tried.

Jesus Himself suffered, and He never promised us an absence of trouble. However, we *are* promised that in the time of trouble, we can hide in the secret place (Ps 91:1). The key is to be able to identify the nature of our trouble and how to respond. Psalm 91:15 instructs us to call upon Him in the day of trouble. He is a very present help, and He is with us. He will answer when we call upon Him.

There is much to consider while reading about the three Israelites Shadrach, Meshach, and Abednego in Daniel chapter 3. They faced a fiery trial with the prospect of being thrown into a fiery furnace. They had determined in their hearts to refuse to bow down to an image of gold and were filled with the faith that God was able to deliver them. No matter the end result, they were fully dedicated to God. They were facing this trial because they did something right, not because they did something wrong.

We all know that it gets hot in the kitchen and that facing trials is not what you want to do on your vacation. However, just as Jesus was with the Israelites, He is with you during fiery trials. Just as their hair and clothing were not singed and they did not smell of smoke, Jesus is with you as you choose to honor God. The fiery trial may not have its origin in God, but the presence of Jesus causes it to work for good. The Israelites emerged from the fire smelling like a rose. God was glorified and they were protected and promoted by the king. This account of commitment to God, fiery trial, and intervention by Jesus is an example for our instruction and benefit.

Crucified with Christ

Promises related to the resurrection and ascension of Jesus Christ seem to be more popular than the death and burial promises of Christ. However, the application of both in our lives has equal value according to my mentor, Pastor Harry T. Goh.

They do not exclude each other, and you can't have one without the other. Jesus said if any man comes after Him, let him take up his cross and follow Him. We have to die to self so we can live; death and burial precede resurrection. We have to die first in order to be resurrected. Dying to self is part of being purified and more like Jesus. When Jesus told us to count the cost, He wasn't just referring to the persecution we may encounter.

God is God of our circumstances. Jesus promises that in this present world *we will* have tribulation, and at the same time He has already won the victory (Jn 16:33). All things, good or bad, work together for the good for those who love God and are called according to His purpose (Rom 8:28). Through all these things we learn to be content in whatever circumstances we are in. It may sometimes feel like God moved to the next county, but He who is Love will never leave or forsake us.

Divine Destiny

Trials are not necessarily proof of judgment or an invitation for us to leave a situation. One way to look at trials is similar to receiving an inoculation. Travel to Third-World countries without proper inoculations can expose us to serious illnesses. Amazingly, these inoculations are limited doses of dormant diseases we are trying to avoid. Some inoculations require a series of shots.

Likewise, we also have a journey to travel in life to fulfill our destiny in God. The Great Physician sometimes inoculates us with a series of circumstances in order to prevent us from being ruined spiritually in the future. Problems we encounter are a priceless part of our heavenly education when we allow God to use them for our good and His glory.

God's purpose in humbling and testing the children of Israel was to develop in them a dependence upon Him and

His Word. He taught them to remember Him and all He had done for them through trying circumstances. God's plan was to prepare them to enter into the land of promise, for them to have longevity and victory and to do them good in the end (Deut 8).

Another example of trials (training) to fulfill one's destiny is the life of David. David was disliked, demeaned, devalued, denied recognition, and dumped in the middle of nowhere by those closest to him. Caring for and protecting his father's sheep was an important part of his training to face Goliath, years of persecution from Saul, and kingship. David's worship and harp playing developed his relationship with God and prepared him to minister to Saul. "David had the anointing of God upon him because of faithfulness in the obscurity in his home life, because there he had passed the test. He was anointed by the Spirit of God alone in private before he came out into the public arena to stand in the name of the Lord."[1]

God can use trials in our lives in the same way He prepared and perfected Joseph. Through a couple of dreams, the Word of the Lord tried Joseph, and he later recognized that God had made him prosperous and fruitful in the land of his affliction. A promise from God can become a test when circumstances persistently appear to contradict God's promise for you. Sometimes, the land of blessing and opportunity can appear to be the land of affliction, and life can become a daily grind. We must keep our eyes on God and believe He is working for us during the "meantime" and moving us toward our divine destiny because He knows the future. Equally, God is able to transform the land of our affliction into the land of our prosperity, as He did with Joseph. Remember the testimony; God's faithfulness is greater than any difficulty.

God, the omnipotent, untiring One, does not become weary in our preparation. He created us in Christ Jesus for good works and prepared the works for us to walk in (Eph 2:10). Our part is to cooperate with Him, depart from sin (2 Tim 2:21), and be a true disciple and learner in the preparation process He has for us. John Wooden, one of the greatest basketball coaches of all time, was quoted as saying, "The time to prepare isn't after you have been given the opportunity. It's long before that opportunity arises. Once the opportunity arrives, it's too late to prepare."[2]

The Meantime

The meantime between calling and commissioning can be a "mean time." Greased tracks are not the most common experience while waiting for God's precious promises to be fully realized. God does not always include a standard warranty that guarantees an exact time and place for fulfillment of His promises.

Walking in the will of God does not exclude spiritual warfare and temptation. The devil will attempt to distract you, discourage you, and take you out. Even Jesus was sent into the desert to face temptation, and we will also face temptation. When He was physically weak, the sinless Son of God was tested in the desert by satan himself. After passing the test, Jesus returned to Galilee in the power of the Holy Spirit, prepared for ministry. Like Jesus, tests, trials, or spiritual warfare, may very well precede promotion in our lives.

The critical issue is choosing God and His ways, again and again and again. Another way to express this is learning to overcome day by day, which results in increased spiritual growth (2 Pet 1:5–11). This includes loving God and others as well as responding to the promptings of God and not our own circumstances. Doing so invites supernatural grace to outlast our circumstances and realize the fulfillment of God's promises. God works in us and develops sanctified intestinal fortitude or holy "guts" within us. This is a form of spiritual training and conditioning. Letting patience have its perfect work develops Godly character, and we will come forth as gold after being tested.

God works in us to will and do *His* good pleasure. Sometimes moving out of our comfort zone is moving into the will of God. God desires to match our willingness with His will and give us the desires of our heart. Abba Father desires that we remain in His loving arms rather than be crushed beneath circumstances.

Here are some things that I remind myself of and do in the meantime: I look to Jesus, my living hope, who is always with me. I focus on being faithful in the small things to pass the test. I keep making hay while the sun shines and do what God has placed before me in the stormy season. I don't allow satan or circumstances to prevent me from doing what God wants me to do. I place my hope in God and His promises rather than tapping my fingers and watching the clock. I remind myself that God is good and I can rest and trust in Him. I hide in Him when calamities come; they will pass by and end. I declare that my change and breakthrough will come, and I refuse to lose heart and lay down in defeat. I take up the whole armor of God and having done all, I continue to *stand* (Eph 6:10–18).

Persecution

Those who live Godly lives in Christ Jesus *will* suffer persecution (2 Tim 3:12). The root issue in persecution is the battle between the Kingdom of light and the kingdom of darkness, not flesh and blood. Jesus told us to love our enemies and pray for those who persecute us. Seeing our adversaries through the blood of Jesus enables us to desire God's best for them. Remember, love is the goal; however, the wisdom of protection may require loving and praying from a distance. There are "barkers and biters." Some barks are worse than their bite, but be aware that some don't bark at all—they just bite!

We cannot always exit the circumstances of persecution. Joseph could not choose when to leave prison, so instead of focusing on someday being freed; he chose to work to bless both the guards and inmates. Prison was an opportunity for Joseph to grow in stature, wisdom, and favor with God and man. It became God's "institution of higher learning" prior to promotion. Joseph was, however, able to run from the advances of Potiphar's wife. It was not Joseph's transgression but his choice to flee from evil that resulted in an additional prison term.

David, the warrior, avoided spears thrown at him, and three times temporarily removed himself from Saul's presence. Later, he took his friend Jonathan's informed advice and permanently avoided Saul. David's love for God and His plan overruled this man of war's natural response in a very real and threatening situation. David did not rely on his instincts but instead he relied on God.

It is unwise to make hasty evaluations of those who persecute you and their spiritual state. Some simply do not know what they are doing. Others may react out of jealousy. Some will hate and speak evil of you. Jesus told us to be happy when we are hated and mistreated, to rejoice when it happens and leap for joy (Lk 6:22–23)!

It is a fact that some individuals have given themselves wholly to evil and are energized and motivated by the evil one. Nevertheless, God-given clear discernment must be exercised to accurately evaluate a person's spiritual state. Despite the reality of evil, God promises to prepare blessings for you in the presence of your enemies (Ps 23:5). This could apply to His sovereign activity and/or to literal proximity. In Psalm 91 He also promises that you shall not be afraid of harm when you dwell in His presence. When we are persecuted or insulted for righteousness, we gain the Kingdom of Heaven and our reward is great in Heaven (Mt 5:10–12).

Comparatively Speaking

Not all things seem good at the moment, but all things work together for good. Our momentary light affliction is working for us to create an exceeding, eternal weight of glory (2 Cor 4:17–19). It is worth remembering that affliction and suffering do not last forever. Calamities *will* pass over us. Indeed, we do walk through the valley of the shadow of death, but we do not set up permanent residence there.

There is a huge difference between surviving an experience and growing through an experience with God. God does call us to change many circumstances with the power and authority He has given us. God also calls us to be changed, radically transformed, by our response to the many circumstances we encounter. Living for God does not insure that thanksgiving, praise, and worship are always effortless. Nevertheless, these three things are keys to growing through an experience with God.

Thanksgiving focuses our hearts and minds on God and His goodness. Worship enables us to connect with God in difficult situations even though worship in the midst of trouble is counter to a natural response. Blessing the Lord at all times involves His praise being continually and in every situation in our mouths (Ps 34:1). This includes times of trouble. We have an invitation to have a supernatural response.

Victory

Since God is for us, who can be against us? When the enemy comes in like a flood, we may experience strong attack, *but* God is still stronger. In the midst of challenging scenarios, God is the answer.

Therefore presuming that trouble always results from sin or God being angry with us is a lie—it is false. Human nature defaults to a simple cause and effect explanation for our experience when the heat is turned up. However, Heaven's nature is to rest in the love of God no matter the circumstance. Even though tribulation and perilous times are foretold in scripture, Jesus told us these things so that in Him we will have peace. He concludes by telling us to be of good cheer; He has overcome the world (Jn 16:33)! God gives wonderful promises to overcomers who, by definition, must triumph in the spirit over tests, obstacles, and enemies. As we become more like Jesus, we overcome. He has won the victory and gladly shares it with us. We are victors, not victims! Practice a winning attitude at all times. Arise, stand, dust yourself off, and walk in the name of Jesus!

Prayer

Praise You, Jesus! Help me draw near and follow You closely. You are always with me. You are for me, so who can be against me? You work all things together for good. Your plans for me are for good, not for evil; for a future and hope. Nothing can separate me from Your love. Thank You for leading me in triumph. I choose You. I rejoice with good cheer and leap for joy! Amen.

six

Yours for the Asking

*For whoever calls upon the name
of the Lord shall be saved.*
Rom 10:13

The following is a testimony from a friend of ours. The molestation started and ended in my tenth year. He was sixteen and I was ten. For some strange reason, I convinced myself that everyone, including all my friends, knew it had happened. I began to live a life of shame, feeling ruined, dirty, and used. For probably ten years afterward, every time there was an awkward silence or someone looked at me intently, I assumed he or she knew about my molestation.

The perpetrator was a close family member, someone who was in the position of protecting me. I had been violated physically, mentally, and emotionally by someone who was supposed to keep me safe!

I was such an innocent kid. I remember that was the same year I found out where babies came from. This person showed me pornography and made me do acts I had never even known about. I wore this shame like a cloak. It became a part of me.

The molestation eventually stopped, and my relative evolved into a much admired member of my family and school. He was popular, smart, kind, and funny, and he became the consummate family man. He was always kind and thoughtful, even toward me. Eventually, I convinced myself that I must have somehow been to blame. He acted as if nothing ever happened. And so did I.

As I grew up, I couldn't shake the feeling of being dirty and at fault. Most confusing to me was that I felt so bad for feeling unwanted when the molestation stopped. Did I enjoy it? Did I invite it? The most difficult thing was I couldn't share with anyone. No one could understand or sympathize with me. No one could be mad on my behalf or change anything for me.

I felt trapped because, by all accounts, this person was shaping up to be a great individual. The dilemma was that I knew what happened was wrong, but I did not want to cause more wrongs by telling everyone what had happened. I also thought they would not believe me, and then what would I do?

This young man grew into a very beloved, respected man. He married and had kids. I loved and admired him for the sacrifices he made for our family over the years. I really thought I had forgiven him and just continued to live as if nothing had ever happened to me.

Another ten years passed. I turned thirty years old. Yet, I was still wearing that cloak of shame. I always felt less than other women. One day on a radio show, I heard that it was estimated one out of every three women is sexually molested during her lifetime. It was chilling to think that two people away from me could be sitting a person with the same experiences as me. This thought grew to the point that, as a thirty-year-old woman, I finally had to admit my deep sadness and shame.

I didn't want to carry it around any longer. I chose to confide in a good friend. She arranged for and took me to see Stuart and Shereen, who ministered in healing broken hearts. I had no idea what it entailed. All I knew was that I needed to be free of this thing I hadn't been able to shake through years of Christianity and positive thinking. I knew I was on the right path, even though it seemed as if I should have already been over this.

We started with prayer, and Stuart explained that I would need God's healing presence and touch in order to heal what had happened. For the first time in my life, I began sharing with Jesus what happened to me all those years before when I was an innocent girl. Stuart encouraged me to ask Jesus questions about my experience, which caused me to look at that part of my life in detail—something I had never done before. I had closed my mind to the horrible details that had happened.

As God surfaced a memory, I was encouraged to ask Jesus to step in and be there with me. We also prayed against the enemy carrying the leftover effects of that sin and shame into my present and future life. Scene after scene I saw myself as that little girl and relived the painful experiences I had forced myself to ignore for twenty years. I wanted to quit many times and just go back to not thinking about it but instead, with each memory, and with my own voice, I asked Jesus to step into the scene.

I even asked Him the question I had often thought about before: "Why didn't You do something? Why did You forsake me, Lord? I was just a little girl." I cried for her, for the little girl I had been. I admitted the wrong of the situation in the presence of two reasonable, objective people who also agreed that it wasn't in my mind—what had happened was wrong. I cried for the little girl who was a victim, and I received Jesus's love as I shared.

I cannot say the process was less than painful. But now I cannot think about it without thinking about how God was able to go into my past, into things others had done to me. I invited Jesus to enter into things that had already happened and heal my heart. I cannot explain it any better than that.

I also cannot explain the freedom I received right after this healing happened. I once felt despised, and now I feel loved. I once felt like a person even God chose to neglect, and now I feel beloved by God. God was there in my situation. Until I asked Jesus questions, I never realized the molestation had ended very abruptly. I still don't know if it was by God's intervention. All-in-all, I want to put it very simply: because of this healing, for the first time in my adult life, I feel like I am a good person.

There is one last twist in this story of my life. It involves the process of forgiving the relative and the people who should have been around to protect me. Exactly two months after my healing, this relative died in a horrible accident. He had been a part of my life every year of my childhood. He lived in our house. We went to the same school. I loved him, and he was part of most of my childhood memories. If God hadn't made me aware of this heavy cloak of shame that caused me to feel so out of place in my life as a Christian, if I had procrastinated by just a few weeks, the events that took place would have compounded my shame.

I don't know why bad things happen to people who do nothing to invoke them. I know one thing in my particular situation, and I hold fast to that. I know the enemy can't accuse this relative whom I loved or me. Jesus had set him free from that by setting me free first. Bottom line, Jesus is still in the business of saving people. God spared me a second cloak of shame and brought me to a place of forgiveness in such a way that I would receive healing as well.

For me, this healing has meant being able to enjoy my womanhood. I write this testimony almost two years after my healing. I am now engaged to a wonderful man. I no longer feel less than other women. My heart is not the same. My heart is now like the girl I was before this all happened. God can do that. I couldn't achieve that for all the education, smarts, and self-analysis I possessed. God can completely heal shattered hearts and revive dreams.

I hope my story of healing encourages you, the reader, to take Jesus into any memory, to take Him into your most secret place, even if you feel you should already be over it. He can change everything and set you free to *really live*. He can make you the person He planned for you to be. I called on the name of the Lord and I was healed!

The Name of Jesus

There is no other name under heaven but Jesus by which a person can be saved (Acts 4:12). The name Jesus literally means, "God is salvation." The name of Jesus, the name above all names, is exceedingly precious. Asking Jesus, yes, even crying out to Him, is scriptural (Ps 88:2–3). A vivid memory of mine is a woman kneeling in church and crying out "Jesus" repeatedly. That dear woman was fully capable of praying another prayer. However, there is no better prayer, none more effective, and none more eloquent than the name of Jesus. Yes, I believe one word; one Name can make us completely whole. To cry, "Help me, Jesus!" is entirely accurate and good, and the Holy Spirit helps us to pray. "If we don't know how or what to pray, it doesn't matter. He does our praying in and for us, making prayer out of our wordless sighs, our aching groans. He knows us far better than we know ourselves" (Rom 8:26–27, The Message).

His Name Is Jesus

His name is Jesus, Jesus.
Sad hearts weep no more.
He has healed the brokenhearted,
Opened wide the prison doors,
He is able to deliver evermore.[1]

Go To the Rock

Prayer points us to a personal encounter and relationship with the Lord Jesus Christ. If we don't expect to encounter the Rock of our salvation when we pray, we deny His nature and desire for relationship. He created us for relationship, and only He can fill the God-shaped hole in each of our hearts. In our deepest valleys, Jesus is the Good Shepherd who leads and comforts us. Jesus, a man acquainted with sorrows, fully understands all of our feelings and experiences.

As we read in chapter 2, Jesus is completely acquainted with you. He has known you since before the world was created, and He formed you in your mother's womb. He identifies with your personal history because He carried away your pain and healed you at the cross. And because Jesus knows you and all you have experienced, He knows exactly how to minister to you. The logical mind might suggest five ways to be healed spiritually, but Jesus ministers directly and hits the nail squarely on the head. As He meets the deepest needs of your heart, it becomes crystal clear that He loves you.

To ask Jesus to heal you is a God thing. "For we do not have a High Priest who cannot sympathize with our weaknesses, but was in all points tempted as we are, yet without sin" (Heb 4:15).

What does this mean? Jesus sits at the right hand of the Father in Heaven and He is deeply touched by our weaknesses, infirmities, and prayers. Not only is He moved by our suffering, but He is also moved to act on our behalf. Jesus was moved with compassion to heal multitudes, and He is moved with compassion to heal each of us today. This is not an attempt to chase Jesus down and get His attention. He loves you, and He is gazing upon you this very moment. Can you ask Jesus to heal you now?

Prayer

Jesus, You are the One I want. You are the One I need. You are here. Love and heal me now. Thank You. Amen.

seven

Freely Receive

Freely you have received,...
Mt 10:8b

The family has gathered. Love and laughter fill the house. The room is warm and the aroma from the kitchen makes you anticipate a feast. The tree is decorated, and it imparts the unique fragrance that recalls feelings and memories of years past. Underneath the tree are beautifully-wrapped gifts that have been repeatedly inspected and shaken.

It is Christmas morning, and you are invited to celebrate Jesus with the family of God. The gift of Christ is for you. You do not have to wait even one more moment to open your gift. By definition, a gift is something freely given! You cannot work for or earn this gift. You are saved (made whole) by grace through faith, and Jesus is the grace gift available to you. This includes forgiveness for *all* your sins and healing for *all* your diseases (Ps 103:3). Today is the day, now is the time, to open the free gift of Jesus and *all* He has for you.

Growing up, my family and I lived on a cul-de-sac in a small town in North Carolina. Our dog, Brownie, was an enthusiastic, energetic cocker spaniel. His obsession was chasing cars, and somehow he frequently succeeded in finding his way to busy streets. Brownie was hit thirteen times in his headlong pursuit of automobiles. Each time we rushed him to the vet or brought him home to bandage his wounds and nurse him back to health. Never did we discuss finding a new home for Brownie, although he repeatedly engaged in risky behavior that caused him substantial injury and pain—not to mention the significant dent he put in my dad's wallet. Brownie was part of our family, and we dearly loved him. God yearns to minister His love, forgiveness, healing, and righteousness to us even when we miss the mark repeatedly.

Asking Jesus for healing might be viewed as "I'm messed up *again*, and I need help from God *again*. Will I ever be healed?" To become obsessed with what you still need healing for is to focus on what you lack instead of focusing on Jesus and all He has accomplished. He is in charge, leading you in the growth, learning, and healing process. Make the most of every opportunity! Jesus is knocking on the door of your heart with love (Rev 3:20), and He is ready to address any area. Open your door for Jesus to enter in.

Encounter Jesus

God offers you the opportunity to encounter Jesus every day. The presence of Jesus and His love enables you to face and conquer whatever devastations you have experienced. You are not facing difficult things alone. He will always be with you. Permit yourself to feel. Jesus came to earth to give you life—life abundant *now*. How do you encounter Jesus? First ask Jesus to meet with you face to face and then allow time for this to happen. If you find yourself getting frustrated, ask for patience and then ask Jesus again! Encounter Jesus, listen to Him, share with Him, and then stay with Him. The Holy Spirit, the Comforter, comes alongside you to help you every step of the way.

One morning as I sought God, I began to express my love to Him. I shared from my heart the love and gratitude I felt for Him. Then I waited quietly and experienced His peace. Afterward, as I continued to be still, I felt two arms embrace me from behind. Then I experienced the sensation of someone's head resting on my right shoulder. Father God came and gave me a big, warm hug that lasted quite awhile!

The Living Christ

Jesus knows each of us through and through, and He loves us beyond understanding. Through a patient, engaging interaction, Jesus revealed Himself as the Messiah to the Samaritan woman at the well. He loves to personally encounter us and have intimate fellowship with us. He does not just give us what we expect but also what we so desperately need. He is not only able to do exceeding and abundantly more than we can ask or think, He *is* so much more than we can ask or think. We have questions and needs, and Jesus is an unlimited, infinite supply for us. He not only has the answer, Jesus is the Answer. Encounter Jesus, the real deal.

Come Boldly

We are invited to enter the holiest place through Jesus. Jesus is the key, the door, the gate, and the way to all of God's goodness and riches. As we enter through Jesus, we draw near to God, and He draws near to us. Another scripture that encourages us to respond to this invitation is found in Hebrews 4:16: "Let us therefore come boldly to the throne of grace that we may obtain mercy and find grace to help in time of need." If we are hurting or sick, it is our time of need. We need help when we need help. Let us come boldly and freely with confidence to God through Jesus and receive what we need.

Do not allow yourself to be held back by past failures or timidity. "Boldness" or "boldly" means we do not have to worry about being received by Abba Father. He receives us when we come to Him. Go directly, with confidence, cheerful courage, and boldness. There is nothing that can prevent us from coming to Abba Father to receive mercy and grace. Our bold, active response in coming to God places us in a perfect position to receive supernatural mercy and grace.

Listen to Him

There was a wedding in Cana of Galilee, and Jesus and His disciples had been invited to attend. At some point in the celebration, the wine ran out. Mary, Jesus's mother, instructed the servants at the wedding, "Whatever He says to you, do it" (John 2:5b). At this point it is important to note that for them to do what Jesus said, they needed to be actively listening to hear Him. Jesus instructed the servants to fill up six water pots with water. Now, it is probable that one or two of the servants had this thought: "Does Jesus really know what He is doing? We don't need water, we need more wine!" As we are actively listening to hear Jesus, we must also respond and do what He says no matter what it looks like, even if you think He's working the "wrong miracle." The result of the servants' listening and obeying allowed them to share in Jesus's first miracle! Water was changed into wine and our lives can be changed in the same way.

Jesus said My sheep hear My voice and follow Me (Jn 10:27). He speaks, but it is beneficial to prepare to hear Him, watch to see what He does, and respond in obedience. Opening your heart and mind to hear is necessary to do the things He says. You were made in God's image, for intimate communication and relationship with Him. He often chooses to speak in extraordinary ways and through unusual means. He uses all of our senses and then some. He sends angels to touch us, to speak to us. He uses colors, sounds, and memories. Everything He desires to use is catered specifically to "speak" to us. God's nature is to communicate. Fundamental to every believer's nature is the ability to "hear" from God. Ask Him, hear Him, follow Him.

Ask to Receive

Rick Taylor and his wife Lori serve as the Divisional Directors for North America for the International Association of Healing Rooms and as the Directors of the Healing Rooms of the Santa Maria Valley. For all the directing they do, they have a great sense of humor to boot! For the past four years I have been privileged to learn and grow from them both. Rick lives, eats, breathes, and preaches the Kingdom of God, and he frequently instructs that *asking* is required to receive the Kingdom of God.

The acronym ASK is an effective way to call these valuable scriptures to mind. Jesus told us to Ask and it will be given; Seek and you will find; Knock and it will be opened to you. Receiving follows asking; finding follows seeking; and opening follows knocking (Mt 7:7–8). We are encouraged by scripture to ask directly. Asking with expectation is an expression of faith that pleases God. James 4:2 states that we have not because we ask not. Putting all this together, it is very clear that we are required to ask in order to receive.

"The effective, fervent prayer of a righteous man avails much" (James 5:16b). The fervent prayer in scripture can be translated as the action of crying out. Crying out or calling out to Jesus functions as an effective prayer. Hannah wept and cried out to God for her womb to be opened and it was opened. Elijah prayed fervently that it would not rain in Israel and it did not rain for three years. Blind Bartimaeus cried out to Jesus to have mercy on him and his sight was restored. It is possible to perceive a person's actions as a disturbance, interruption, inconvenience, or embarrassment, while Jesus might see it as asking to receive! Or more specifically, we are asking for God's Kingdom in heaven to come down right now here on earth. Asking is not begging, but it is honestly pouring out one's heart to God.

Do you want to really live full of joy? Ask Jesus to do whatever it takes. To ask Jesus to do all He wants to do invites the exceeding abundance of God into your life. Ask Him to heal you to the maximum 100 percent. Ask Him to intervene and completely override your control. Rest in Him, hear His Words, and see what He is doing. Trust God and His perfect love once again today. Thank God as He heals you and give Him praise! And then encourage yourself to continue!

Prayers

> ➤ Abba Father, what are Your thoughts toward me?
> ➤ What do I feel anxious and worried about?
> ➤ What do You want to heal me of?

eight

Agreement and Assistance

Again I say to you that if two of you agree on earth concerning anything that they ask, it will be done for them by My Father in heaven.
Mt. 18:19

Four men carried the paralytic onto the roof, created an opening, and lowered their friend to Jesus. The planning and effort that they exerted was intended to position their paralyzed friend squarely before the Healer. They knew who Jesus was, where He was, and the healing He carried. The four men loved their paralyzed friend, and their assistance placed him before The Healer. They had hoped and likely prayed for an opportunity for the paralytic to be healed and had agreed among themselves to help him prior to this time. Acting quickly and decisively indicates they worked together in unity as a team (Mk 2:1–12, Lk 5:17–26).

Just as God used the four men to place the paralytic before Jesus, He uses individuals and teams to minister healing today. Simply put, God uses people and He works through human beings! And people who are paralyzed—spiritually, mentally, physically, or emotionally—need help not only from God but also from other people.

Agreement

"Again I say to you that if two of you agree on earth concerning anything that they ask, it will be done for them by My Father in heaven" (Mt 18:19). Yes, our first agreement *is* with God and His Kingdom's purposes. Also, the prayer of agreement between people as written in Matthew carries with it Jesus's promise that it will be done by God. One more thing concerning agreement: God commands His blessing when believers dwell together in unity (Ps 133). It is clear in scripture that singleness of purpose produces powerful results. Jesus forgave and healed the paralytic in recognition of the faith of his four friends. God still sends help today through people who are very human.

Receiving the free gift of God includes cooperating with Him and obeying Him. Have you ever felt like Naaman, the Syrian, who was instructed to go to the Jordan River and wash seven times (2 Kgs 5)? He had leprosy, an incurable disease, and he expressed his frustration, saying, "Aren't the rivers in my country better than the river here?" He was weary of pursuing his healing. He may have thought, "I've come all this way and you tell me to wash in this filthy river seven times and I'll be healed? The anointed man of God didn't even bother to come to see me in person! Do you know how many things I've tried already? My entire life has been consumed with this disease." Eventually, Naaman heeded the encouragement of his servant and performed the Word of the Lord from Elisha. Even after getting advice from his trusted servant, Naaman had to choose to obey the Word of the Lord to receive His healing.

Peculiar People

Have you cried out to God for more revelation, healing, deliverance, or a radical change in your life? God may minister to you directly or He may send someone to minister to you. He may ask you to visit a person or place outside your home church or denomination. The bride of Christ is not housed in one church building, and the river of God is not confined to a single stream. God makes no guarantee that the type of person He chooses to minister to you will be what you are accustomed to. From my experience, some of the most refreshing, impacting, and loving persons are anything but "ordinary."

Knowing God's heart enables us to see as God sees because man looks on the outward appearance, but God looks on the heart. Jesus was not the anticipated Messiah "package" many expected. He was despised and rejected by those who demanded that He meet their every personal expectation. We are blessed when we choose not to be offended by Jesus and what He does. It is possible to miss a significant blessing of God by critically judging the outer appearance. If we are seeking God and His Word, we are able to rightly divide the Word of truth, no matter from what cloth the messenger is cut.

He Chooses Whom He Uses

In the 1970s God mercifully gave me the grace to return to Him. My outward appearance revealed a young man pummeled by sin and ungodly choices, but God looks on the heart. Father God welcomed me as a returning prodigal son and gave me a passion for healing. Soon after returning to the Lord, I visited a school counselor who was in the hospital awaiting surgery to remove a brain tumor. He expressed fear that if the surgery was unsuccessful, the two young boys he had recently adopted would be placed in foster care. I asked if I could pray for him, and then I touched him lightly on the forehead and prayed briefly. Afterward he shared that he felt peace. A scan immediately prior to scheduled surgery the next morning revealed no trace of a brain tumor. Surgery was cancelled. Dr. Jesus had already operated.

Bella

In my personal experience, God has at times chosen unusual ways to minister to me. While my sons were elementary-school age, they prayed daily for three years, "Jesus, give us a dog!" During a particularly hard season in my life, when I returned home from travel, I discovered a little red dog had been given to our family. At first I wondered why a wiener dog (official breed name dachshund) had come into our lives, but I soon discovered the reason. During this time, our little red dog kept me company. Every day she lay with her head on my shoulder while I sought God. She attentively listened to me as I cried out to God. My experience is just one of the many ways God expresses His love. His ministry to me through little Bella during a very difficult time kept my heart soft and my faith childlike.

How Much?

How much do you want healing and wholeness? How much do you want the Healer? Surrender control to God. You do not have to understand everything He does before you allow Him to heal you. If you hunger and thirst after righteousness (Jesus), you *will* be filled (Mt 5:6). You have a choice: sincerely ask God to heal you and cooperate with Him or spend your time attempting to instruct Him how to do what only He can do.

Even though healing is what we are after, the healing process itself can feel anything but comfortable. Deep healing may not be your first choice for a leisure activity, but the end result is rewarding in both the short and long term. Inconvenient situations can be profitable when God uses them to uncover things that lead to your healing. Choose to face difficult circumstances when God desires to reveal something that will bring healing to you.

Accountability

Accountability groups are valuable, particularly when the focus is God! Praying and encouraging others to follow God's path is biblical and effective. A healthy accountability group breathes life into and fans the flame for a personal relationship with God. This means honesty and transparency must be practiced in order for this type of ministry to be effective. Confessing our sins to one another and praying for one another results in healing (Jas 5:16).

Accountability systems or groups, however, were never meant to replace personal heart work with God. Vertical accountability (man to God) and a relationship with the Word are absolutely necessary to live in the Truth. Each person ultimately answers to God, and because our first relationship is with Him, our first accountability is to Him.

My Way or the "High Way"

Demanding that God minister in a certain way does not limit God. He has all the goods. Demanding that God minister in a certain way does, however, prevent us from receiving all that He has for us. Focusing on a single perception instead of God Himself can cause us to miss God entirely. God does what He wants to do however He wants to do it. He makes a way where there is no way. God has perfect love and a perfect plan for you.

Blessed Precondition

Jesus said, "Freely you have received, freely give." As you receive, God places a heavenly deposit within you that can be drawn from and given away. Receiving is one prerequisite for giving Jesus's healing salvation to others. You can easily give what you have received from God in love, healing, anointing, and passion. You can also minister healing by exercising belief, faith, spiritual gifts, and obedience.

Prayer

God, You have perfectly fit together every part of the body of Christ to minister life to the other parts. I gratefully receive all the divine help You provide both directly from You and through earthen vessels. Every good and perfect gift is from You. Thank you, Jesus. Amen.

nine

Freely Give

Freely you have received, freely give.
Mt 10:8b

Pastor Harry Goh, my mentor, once asked me, "Which fits better, a readymade or a custom-made suit?" Although I don't wear suits all that often, I have been to a tailor and I appreciate the art and finesse that is put into making a custom suit. A custom-made, tailored suit is specifically made for a specific person using precise measurements and attention to detail. A readymade suit, on the other hand, is made to fit the standard form. However, there are very few people who can put on a readymade suit and find it needs no alterations.

Authentic Kingdom ministry is similar to a custom-tailored suit. Our loving Father specifically and precisely ministers in a way that fits each of us just like a tailored suit. In the context of intimate personal fellowship with God, He also deposits within each of us what we need to minister to other individuals as well. This is not guesswork or always using a default ministry protocol; it is drawing from the mind of Christ in us. If we follow a procedural list and it is the Word of God, it has great value. However, ministering from a cookie cutter list of endlessly repeated procedures is far less effective than presenting the person with fresh information from Jesus. He has *more* than a readymade suit (a list) to minister to those He loves. To minister healing is to carry His very presence. It is the fruit of an ongoing intimate relationship with Him.

Jesus's biblical example was, "I do what I see the Father do," (Jn 5:19) and, "I say what I hear the Father say" (Jn 12:49–50). This is the model that Jesus ministered from. Jesus is our example, and when we do it the way He did it, we are inviting the Kingdom of God to come and God's will to be done. Another application of hearing and seeing is written in Habakkuk: "I will stand my watch And set myself on the rampart, And watch to see what He will say to me,…" (Hab 2:1). Therefore it is possible to *hear* by *seeing* or even *see* by *hearing*. Seeing and hearing are means by which God can communicate and give us understanding.

You can follow Jesus's example because He no longer calls you a servant who does not know what the master is doing. A servant serves out of obedience in response to commands. Jesus calls us friends, and all the things He has heard from the Father, He makes known to us (Jn 15:15). Being a friend of Jesus is a fellowship of love with Him that opens an access to what the Father is *doing* and *saying*. Receiving manna, fresh heavenly bread, is a matter of daily gathering and stepping out in faith to use what God gives you. We are chosen and appointed as friends who partner with Him in Kingdom activities. Saying what we hear God say is to speak words that impart life. As we cooperate with what God says and does, Kingdom purposes are accomplished.

His Glory

The glory of God is the manifest or visible presence of God that reveals His character and nature. In the Old Testament, Moses asked for God's presence to go with him. Moses then asked God to show him His glory, and Moses saw all of God's goodness as His glory passed before him. Through this we see that Moses also became a carrier of God's glory (Ex 33–34). In the glory realm, the supernatural atmosphere of heaven (God) becomes tangible (touchable) on earth.

In the New Testament, Jesus, the King of Glory, came from heaven to earth to reveal God. Jesus is the very expression and image of God on this earth. He was transfigured, and the glory shone from His face like the sun (Mt 17:1–13). To encounter the glory of God, we must encounter the God of glory. We *can* ask, see, and carry His glory.

Jesus promises to share His glory with us (Jn 17:5–6, 20-26). As the Head of the church, He fills His body with His fullness. In the glory where His goodness is displayed, sovereign, supernatural activity occurs, whereby we are transformed from glory to glory into the image of Christ (2 Cor 3:17–18). We can carry His glory naturally as a result of His supernatural work within us.

Belief and Faith

Let's take a look at scriptures that address the benefits of believing. *Believe* in the Lord Jesus Christ, and you will be saved, you and your household (Acts 16:31). If you confess with your mouth the Lord Jesus and *believe* in your heart that God has raised Him from the dead, you will be saved (Rom 10:9). To do the works of God, *believe* in Jesus, the one God sent (Jn 6:28–29). Jesus promised that if you *believe* in Him, supernatural signs will follow you (Mk 16:14–20). God backs up His commission with exceeding greatness of power toward us who *believe* (Eph 1:19–20). Jesus promised that if you *believe* in Him, you will do the same works and greater works than He did (Jn 14:12). Jesus said that if you *believe*, you will see the glory of God (Jn 11:40).

And now faith...*faith* is seeing the unseen. *Faith*, then, is a confident assurance in God and all that He says, not just what we see with our natural eyes (Heb 11:1). If we have *faith* as a tiny mustard seed we can move mountains and all things are possible (Mt 17:20). God has given each of us a measure of *faith* (Rom 12:3). Without *faith* it is impossible to please God (Heb 11:6). This truth might also be expressed simply as *faith* pleases God. Is it possible *we* are the ones limiting God? What? To limit God by a lack of faith really makes no sense!

In a nutshell this is how I see it: belief and faith go hand in hand. If I believe in Jesus and all that He said and did while on this earth, and my faith is at least the size of a mustard seed, then I can move any mountain.

Gifts and Anointing

Spiritual gifts are gifts of the Holy Spirit as described in 1 Corinthians 12:1–11.[1] These Holy Spirit gifts are given to help us continue Jesus's work on earth. They are given and are meant to be used and not hidden away or warehoused. These spiritual gifts are intended to always be ministered with and drenched in love.

Jesus was anointed with the Holy Spirit without measure. Pastor Harry Goh states: "We need more than teaching alone, we need the gifts and anointing of the Holy Spirit *activated*." The anointing glorifies Jesus and is a testimony of Him. The anointing breaks every yoke of bondage. Jesus said the Spirit of the Lord is upon me because He has anointed me... (Lk 4:18). The fulfillment of His mission on earth depended upon Jesus being anointed with the Holy Spirit.

Each of us needs all of God and all of Heaven we can get on earth. This includes what Jesus presented to John the Baptist as proof of His being the Anointed One: "The blind see, the lame walk, the lepers are cleansed, and the deaf hear; the dead are raised up and the poor have the gospel preached to them" (Mt 11:5). God is ready to give you good and perfect gifts, anointing, and the Kingdom of Heaven. It is the Father's good pleasure to give you the Kingdom. God is so very ready to bless you and others through you! Ask for spiritual gifts that express the love of God in a tangible way. Then minister the gifts in the Holy Spirit to convey love and healing.

It's All Good

The solution is not choosing *between* but instead choosing all of the above. God's sovereign activity and glory, belief and faith, and gifts and anointing are all part of ministering to others. His glory, faith, and gifts were never intended to function separately. Each is of God, each is invaluable. Choose all of the above. God is eager to share what He says and does because of His great love.

Healing Is Simple

At a recent Healing the Brokenhearted training seminar, a practical question was asked: "What is the protocol, the procedure for ministering healing to the brokenhearted?" My immediate answer was, "Jesus is the protocol, the procedure, the one step necessary in healing." First ask Jesus and then rest in His presence. Proceed according to what He says and does. Doing what Jesus indicates is following His lead, order, and timing. Encountering Jesus and responding to Him is the key. The following testimony demonstrates how simple and easy healing is when we encounter Jesus:

I attended a Healing the Brokenhearted session at the Healing Rooms of the Santa Maria Valley after my husband of twenty-two years filed for divorce. Stuart and Shereen guided me through breaking unhealthy soul ties from older relationships. They ended by asking me to place my hand over my heart, and they placed their hands on mine and prayed for God to heal my shredded heart. As we sat and prayed, I felt heat surround my heart. God was cauterizing my wounds and healing my scars. The heat continued for several hours after the session, and then a great peace and joy descended upon me. I have gone from brokenhearted to hopeful and joyful!

The Basics

Many individuals have already heard from Jesus and simply don't recognize it is Him. They perceive it as their own personal thoughts or imagination. God created our imagination, and He can communicate with us, His creation, any way He desires. It can benefit people to encourage them to share things they perceive but may not initially understand. Following Jesus is expressing what is sensed, felt, smelled, experienced, known, seen, heard, imagined, dreamed of, envisioned, etcetera. This can be a starting point. In my experience, often the very first thing that crosses a person's mind is from Jesus. Most people who "just can't hear from Jesus" *do hear* when they simply relax in His presence. I have also found that worship definitely facilitates receiving and hearing.

Words of knowledge and revelation received by the person who is ministering do not have to be immediately shared. If the Holy Spirit gives a word of knowledge to the person ministering, He is also able to give that same word of knowledge to the person who is being ministered to. Jesus wants to minister directly and personally to the person who has the need. Let what the Holy Spirit reveals to you, the minister, gently shape the direction or type of question you guide the person to ask Jesus directly. The will of our Father is fulfilled, not frustrated, by guiding others to go boldly to Jesus for communication, revelation, and deep personal ministry. Point people to Jesus, and they will have more than an answer to their question. They will receive *The Living Word*. Jesus not only has the answer to their question, He *is* the Answer!

Meekness

"Take My yoke upon you, and learn of Me; for I am meek and lowly in heart, and ye shall find rest unto your souls" (Mt. 11:29 KJV). The nature and prominent characteristic of a meek person is restfulness, exercising gentleness through being quiet. A meek person refrains from offering excessive information as a form of courtesy, respect, and honor. Another way of putting this is a meek person exercises great restraint in saying things that could be helpful in another's life, instead allowing time for others to pursue God for themselves and seek out further details from Him directly. Ministering in meekness demonstrates love, which builds a person up.

Can You Ask Jesus?

Jesus is the Alpha and the Omega, the beginning and the end. As I mentioned earlier in chapter six, the name Jesus means, "God is salvation." Another of His names, Immanuel, means "God with us." Salvation is a person who is always there for us. When we ask Jesus, we are seeking a face-to-face encounter with Him. To ask Jesus places an expectation directly on His love, anointing, and miracle healing power.

Jesus is, in fact, the Healer. To come boldly and ask Jesus is cutting to the chase—the bottom line. Rather than focusing on the problem(s), asking Jesus what He wants to do is pressing into the Solution. Since Jesus has all the answers to every problem, it makes sense to ask what He wants to share. Knowing every detail of the problem is unnecessary when you already have Jesus, the Answer. He has the key to every heart. The result could be gradually unfolding revelation or an awesome transformation at the speed of light!

There are many ways to minister healing. The goal of asking Jesus is not to "turn over every rock." The goal is encountering Jesus the Healer and Jesus the Answer, who is always available. The objective is to turn over *the* rock that Jesus wants to work on. Then the person can continue going to Jesus and receiving what is needed. We do not need to get a jackhammer out and turn over every bit of concrete. Jesus has a way of showing each of us what He wants because He knows how much we can handle at that particular time. I believe the reason the Lord taught us to pray, "Give us this day our daily bread," is because He has portioned out for us what He wants us to look at for that day. If we are willing to minister by following the Holy Spirit's lead, we will teach people how to connect with Jesus and they can follow His lead as well. To point others to Jesus honors Him and connects people more closely with Him. It equips and empowers them to go to the Source. Teaching a man to fish is more valuable than giving a man a fish. The goal of teaching to ask and encounter Jesus is receiving a lifetime of bread from heaven instead of a single slice of bread.

How To

For the person's initial contact, set them at ease right away— let him or her know the goal in healing the brokenhearted is encountering Jesus, who loves them very much. You are affording them additional time for the purpose of hearing from Jesus directly. What if he or she comes in with a premade list of prayer needs? Let them know you are concerned with his or her needs (list) but sometimes Jesus has a different plan. Ask if they are willing to explore what He wants to do. The person may declare that he or she doesn't "hear" from Jesus, or when they've tried in the past, it just ended in frustration. They want answers now! The key is to help him or her relax and allow the Holy Spirit to rest on them. An effective prayer at this point is to command frustration and anything blocking or hindering the person from hearing Jesus, to *GO!* (as in leave immediately)

The following are several things I often do while ministering healing to the brokenhearted. This is not meant to be an order of operation or an exhaustive list.

- Allow Jesus to direct and set the pace.
- Plant the seed, the encouraging Word of God, in the person.
- Remind the person of their identity in Christ.
- Bless and express the love of the Father to the person.
- Invite the Holy Spirit and wait for His ministry.
- Encourage the person to ask Jesus out loud directly for encounter, revelation, and healing.
- Allow time for the person to hear directly and report what Jesus is doing.
- Step into power and authority to remove obstacles and hindrances to seeing or hearing from God.
- Free the person out of pits and places of bondage and then connect them with Jesus.
- Suggest questions the person may ask Jesus about the revelation they have received.
- Share when appropriate, what Jesus has revealed to you. Ask, "Does that mean something to you?" and/or "Can you ask Jesus what that means?"
- Fill the person with healing in body, soul, spirit, love, and the goodness of God.
- Seal the person with the body and blood of Jesus.
- Give the person scripture and information that will build them up, help them stand, and keep their healing
- If the person is struggling to encounter Jesus, encourage them and offer help in the form of a question they can

ask Jesus directly. For example, here are some sample questions I would suggest to the person. Can you ask Jesus:

➢ "Jesus, come and encounter me now."
➢ "Jesus, come and love me."
➢ "Jesus, come and minister to me."
➢ "Jesus, what do You want to do?"
➢ "Jesus, what do You have to say?"
➢ "Jesus, what do You think about me?"
➢ "Jesus, what do You want to show or reveal to me?"
➢ "Jesus, what is the truth and what is the lie?"
➢ "Jesus, what do I feel?"
➢ "Jesus, why do I feel (ie, angry)?"
➢ "Jesus, what do You want to give me?"
➢ "Jesus, shine Your light in me."

Provide the person an opportunity to hear from Jesus and then allow him or her to share what He is doing. Wait for a while instead of rushing to another question. Wait until he or she receives a "word." This does not necessarily mean a complete prophetic word but perhaps a simple "clue" that helps them move forward. Allow the person to experience the joy of receiving from and responding to Jesus and developing an increasingly intimate relationship with Him.

As we work toward healing in body, soul, and spirit, wounds must be cleaned, just as physicians thoroughly clean wounds after surgery. We can pour the blood of Jesus over the person and their wounds. Jesus's blood ministers forgiveness, healing, deliverance, and everything the person needs.

As you minister to the person, here are some more questions you may suggest:

➢ "Can you ask Jesus to help you forgive?"
➢ "Jesus, come take my pain and heal me."

> "Jesus, what do you want to give me in exchange for the pain You just took away?"
> "Jesus, fill me with Your love, joy, peace, and hope."

Stand

What happens if the person you are ministering to strays off course while asking Jesus? The person probably does not need a word of correction; you can simply ask him or her, "What else is Jesus showing you?" What if the person shares a word that doesn't line up with the truth? You may also share a scripture that offers truth and hope, pointing them in a positive direction. God's Word is powerful, positive and practical, and provides an opportunity to know God's heart and obey the truth. If the person remains resistant, a good question to ask is: "Can you change your opinion to agree with God?"

What if you run into an obstacle or a road block that continues to be troublesome? Assuming you are praying with a team, allow another team member to minister. However, if a person is not ready to address the obstacle or road block, don't force it. Suggest a follow-up appointment when he or she is ready. Asking Jesus is valuable because it focuses on The Solution. Ministering in Kingdom power and authority will be addressed in the next chapter.

Prayer

Jesus, I have received from You, now I choose to point others to You and Your goodness, and give to them what You have placed within me. I love You, Jesus. Amen.

ten

Power and Authority

Then He called His twelve disciples together and gave them power and authority over all demons and to cure diseases. He sent them to preach the kingdom of God and to heal the sick.
Lk 9:1–2

Jesus has commissioned us to do impossible things with supernatural results. How on earth are we going to accomplish this? Better yet, how are we going to accomplish this on earth?

Power

The essence or nature of all that Jesus has commissioned requires us to step into Kingdom power. This dynamite power (dunamis) Jesus is offering to give us is the Holy Spirit. In John 20:21–22, soon after His resurrection, Jesus revealed Himself to His disciples in the room where they were hiding. This is what He told them: "Peace to you! As the Father has sent Me, I also send you." And when He had said this, He breathed on them and said to them, "Receive the Holy Spirit." In Acts 1:4–5, 8 we also see that Jesus did not want His disciples to immediately set out to fulfill the great commission. He commanded them not to depart from Jerusalem but to wait for the promise of the Father, the baptism of the Holy Spirit. Why did He tell His disciples to do this? Because He knew the power they were to receive was essential and would enable them to do what He had commissioned them to do.

Authority

Jesus said all authority (exousia) had been given to Him (Mt 28:18). Then He gave us what He Himself had been given: God's *all* authority. This authority gives us the right, or the say-so, to use God's power and to act on His behalf.

One example of authority that has been widely shared for many years is that of a policeman. If a person stands in the middle of a busy intersection without a uniform and badge, passing motorists will not recognize and obey the commands he attempts to enforce. If, however, a policeman wears his uniform with his badge, he can stand in the middle of that very same busy intersection and passing motorists will obey his commands. The power and authority that Jesus gave us is over more than just traffic. This power and authority is over all demons and all diseases.

Jesus Our Example

At His baptism, Jesus received the power of the Holy Spirit. His identity as the beloved Son of God was reaffirmed and God's authority was fully released upon Him (Mt 3:16–17). Jesus was anointed to heal and set people free because the Spirit of the Lord was upon Him.

Fulfilling the great commission of Jesus is contingent upon receiving the power of the Holy Spirit and the authority He gives us as sons and daughters of God. The love God has for us leads us into personal revelation of "sonship" (being a son or daughter of God as described in Chapter 3). Sonship allows us to fully receive the authority He has given us. This authority of God licenses us, certifies us, authorizes us, and frees us to fully exercise the power of the Holy Spirit. You were born (again) for this—it is your destiny. When you know who you are, you can be who you are.

He Sent Them

Jesus sent His twelve disciples to preach the Kingdom of God and heal the sick. Preaching refers to the proclamation, that is, the announcing of the presence of the Kingdom of God. Healing the sick is a demonstration of the presence of the Kingdom of God (Lk 9:1–2). A second account of Jesus sending the twelve (Mt 10:7–8) included His instruction to preach as you go, saying the Kingdom of Heaven is near you. In other words, Heaven is here and near to you now. This proclamation contradicts the lie that Heaven is so separated from us in time and space that it is inaccessible now. Jesus told us to demonstrate the Kingdom and the rule and reign of God by freely healing the sick, cleansing lepers, raising the dead, and casting out demons. In this the King and His Kingdom are both proclaimed and demonstrated.

As described in Luke chapter 11, Jesus taught the disciples to pray for the Kingdom of God to come and His will to be done on earth as it is in Heaven. All of Heaven has not come to earth at this point in time. However, Heaven's fullness and best has already come in Jesus. It is obvious that for Heaven to increasingly come to earth, we must exercise our privilege of pulling more of heaven to earth. We actually carry and become "Kingdom" in the deepest sense possible as we pull down Heaven's fullness.

Jesus is the Kingdom package who contains not only what He said and did, but also all He is, which includes perfect love. Rick Taylor often shares both at the Healing Rooms and abroad, speaking about God's love anointing. He encourages us to pray not for the healing anointing, although that's what the Healing Rooms is all about—healing! Instead, Rick encourages us to pray for the love anointing. I highly value this simple yet profound statement he makes: "If God can trust you with His love anointing, He can trust you with His power."

Stepping into Power and Authority

Jesus focused His disciples on God and the Kingdom of God, not on circumstances. He drew their attention away from worry and fear to the goodness, love, and generosity of God. The goal of the one ministering is to assist people who have difficulty looking past their immediate circumstances and to help them access God and His goodness.

When people are unable to free themselves, the person ministering takes a much more active role. Since you know Jesus has given you Kingdom power and authority, it is unnecessary to determine if God wants to heal. God would not invest His power and authority in us so we could just turn away and not use it for His glory. God wouldn't give us His power and authority to heal if He didn't want people healed. That makes no sense and is contrary to God's heart and nature! The power and authority we step into frees the person to do more in personally pursuing Jesus. Check regularly to determine if people are ready to participate more actively in their own healing. The goal for the person receiving ministry is to encounter Jesus, receive His healing, and begin to exercise the power and authority He has granted them.

Removing Obstacles

Removing obstacles includes using the Kingdom keys of binding and loosing (Mt 16:19). Binding evil addresses the root and fruit of evil. If weeds represented evil, the way to get rid of weeds is to pull them out by the roots instead of repeatedly mowing them down. We energetically press into the Kingdom of God by binding evil, and when the obstacle is removed, we are able to loose people.

Removing obstacles also enables a person to receive from Jesus more deeply. For example, as we bind evil and loose Heaven, fear is replaced by perfect love, guilt is replaced by forgiveness, and shame is replaced by honor. Reproach is replaced with grace, favor, and destiny. (The term "reproach" can be used to encompass criticism, rejection, character assassination, judgment, blame, accusations, lies, and all manner of negativity.) Oppression is replaced with freedom; regret is replaced with hope. The sting of death is replaced by the resurrection, life, and victory given to us through our Lord Jesus Christ (1 Cor 15:56–57).

Activate the Exchange

We have the God-given privilege of removing the obstacles that are contrary to the Kingdom of God and blessing with the benefits of Heaven. Eugene Peterson expresses it this way: "And that's not all. You will have complete and free access to God's kingdom, keys to open any and every door: no more barriers between heaven and earth, earth and heaven. A yes on earth is yes in heaven. A no on earth is no in heaven" (Mt. 16:19, The Message). Part of this blessing is calling back the damaged parts of the person to be healed, then blessing the person with all things new, all things restored in the name of Jesus. Establish

the person's entire body, soul, and spirit in heavenly places.[1]
(1 Th 5:23-24, Ps 23, Eph 1:3, 19-20, and 2:6)

God has also bestowed upon each person the responsibility and authority to steward the personal health of his or her own body, soul, and spirit. God's will is that we have life and wholeness. Every child of God has the privilege to access the exchange accomplished at Calvary. He has given each of us the authority to "call back," regain, or reclaim what is our own. He has empowered us to seek, find, and restore that which has been lost or stolen from our body, soul and spirit. This is the time to use your mind, will, and emotions in the authority God has given you to verbally call these things back. Yes, call them back! Reclaim each one. This is part of restoring your soul, restoring what the locusts ate, and restoring your health, your confidence, your joy, your innocence, your relationships, etcetera. You can regain possession of what you once thought would be missing forever by demanding that it be returned. Verbally declare: "I take ____ back in the name of Jesus!" Bless with healing the damaged parts of your soul that have been returned. This is both biblical and empowering.

Prayer

Jesus, thank you for giving us Your power and authority to bind evil, loose people, and bring Heaven to earth. Amen.

eleven

The Pits

Save me, O God!
For the waters have come up to my neck.
I sink in deep mire,
Where there is no standing;
I have come into deep waters,
Where the floods overflow me.
I am weary with my crying;
My throat is dry;
My eyes fail while I wait for my God.
Ps 69:1–3

There are countless people in a hole, literally in a pit. Destructive experiences can exert a lingering and painful influence. These experiences can include abandonment, abortion, abuse in positions of power and authority, bullying, crime, divorce, emotional abuse, sexual abuse, incest, neglect, physical abuse, physical injury, or PTSD from a multitude of stressful situations (this is by no means an exhaustive list).

God's heart is grieved to see suffering when Jesus has already suffered and died to purchase true freedom for mankind. People, the object of God's love, often need help getting free from pits such as sin, bondage, disease, hurt, infirmity, and affliction. Many people lay paralyzed, imprisoned, and immobilized in these pits. How can someone be in a pit when an event occurred months, years, and even decades ago? Individuals can become "stuck" when the destructive past continues to be their present experience. Fear, guilt, shame, and distrust of God, self, and others are common responses of people who are in the pits. These responses cause individuals to experience pain, distraction, and false perceptions. The pain from the past needs to be removed and replaced so that negative feelings and involuntary reactions are no longer a person's current experience.

Pit Stops

In Psalm 40:1–2 David experienced what it was like to be removed from a pit: "I waited patiently for the Lord; and He inclined to me, and heard my cry. He also brought me up out of a horrible pit, Out of the miry clay, and set my feet upon a rock, and established my steps." In Genesis chapter 37, Jacob's son Joseph was literally thrown into a pit by his brothers. God spared his life, and he was sold as a slave and taken to Egypt.

An important part of Jesus's ministry as written in Isaiah 61:1 and Luke 4:18–19 is pulling people out of captivity and opening prison doors. As you give others a hand out of the pit, you are catalytically connecting them with Jesus the Healer. Both a hand out of the pit and a hand up to God are priceless.

To minister to those in the "pits," it is often appropriate to step into power and authority (covered in chapter 10) so they can be freed to do more for themselves. When people are unable to free themselves from a pit, the person ministering becomes more active, ministering more of God's love, removing more obstacles, and pouring in more of God's goodness.

Check regularly to find out if they are ready to participate more actively in their own healing. The goal for the one receiving ministry is to encounter Jesus and receive His healing.

If someone is stuck in a pit and he or she isn't making progress, you can help the person get unstuck by asking questions like Jesus did. Jesus asked questions while He healed. I believe the reason He did this was to get the person's focus off of the pain and begin to activate his or her faith. As you ask questions, people can, by faith, choose to release the pain, embrace Jesus, and receive healing. Let's look at how Jesus activated faith by the questions He asked.

Jesus's Questions

Blind Bartimaeus cried out to Jesus for mercy. Jesus heard his cries for mercy and answered him with a question. I believe Jesus saw exactly what Bartimaeus needed; however, He activated the man's faith by asking, "What do you want Me to do for you?" Bartimaeus answered Jesus, asking to receive his sight. Jesus responded immediately by healing him (Mk 10:46–52).

We can ask the same question today as Jesus asked Bartimaeus. As you minister, encourage the person to verbally address Jesus directly: "Can you tell Jesus what you want Him to do for you?"

Jesus asked the man with an infirmity at the pool of Bethesda, "Do you want to be made well?" (Jn 5:1–15) It was obvious he needed healing because he was lying with the hopelessly sick. The man's initial answer was that there was no man to help him get into the water. By asking this question, Jesus was taking the man's focus off the help of man, self-pity, and affliction and redirecting his focus toward the healing salvation directly in front of him.

As ministers we too should be asking questions that redirect a person's focus off his or her problem and onto Jesus. A prime time to receive healing continues to be during interactions and encounters with Jesus, and asking questions facilitates these encounters!

The habits of years of infirmity require changes in the way people think and in the way people live life. Jesus's instruction to the man at the pool of Bethesda was rise, take up your bed, and walk. It was a prescription from the Great Physician; a call to the obedience of faith and an activation of healing. Doing whatever Jesus says ushers in benefits and miracles.

If the response to God is "No" or "I don't know," identify the issue as a possible obstacle to healing and as something that they can choose to address. Invite the person to ask Jesus to help them be willing to be willing. Express the goodness and willingness of Jesus to heal, and free him or her to receive. If the person is simply not ready, seal the work that has already been done. Welcome a return for further ministry when they decide to proceed. This approach engages the person's will, which in turn helps the person choose to walk it out as a lifestyle and not a one-time event.

One objection to asking a question is that a person may hide the truth or brazenly lie. Of course this can occur in any aspect of life. The minister's responsibility is to present people to Jesus with love. The person's responsibility is to seek an encounter with Jesus and healing with their whole heart. If the person is not ready, healing cannot be forced. If the truth is hidden or deceit is an obstacle, discernment and words of knowledge can reveal this. Even with revelation, however, you cannot override a person's will. The truth will set people free if it goes beyond head knowledge and lip service. Sincerity of heart invites the Truth, who is full of grace and truth, to heal.

Today the world searches for real answers to real problems. Apart from the presence and power of God, deep root issues will not be addressed, nor will true freedom be ministered. Receiving the invaluable presence of Jesus results in deep healing. Once strongholds and everything that exalts itself against the knowledge of Christ are removed and replaced with Jesus, captives are set free.

Psychiatric care and medical care are also valuable resources when necessary. There are anointed Christian medical doctors, psychiatrists, and therapists who are used by God in healing. Common sense and good judgment are necessary in developing a healthy lifestyle, maintaining health, and walking in healing.

Prayer

Jesus, my Savior, I reach out to You. Pull me out of the pit and make me whole. Thank You. Amen.

twelve

Healing from Oppression

How God anointed Jesus of Nazareth with the
Holy Spirit and with power, who went about
doing good and healing all who were oppressed
by the devil, for God was with Him
Acts 10:38

This chapter by no means is an exhaustive study of deliverance. There are numerous authors and titles that address deliverance ministry more thoroughly. What I share in this chapter are a few fundamental tools that I have learned through ministering healing to the brokenhearted.

Throughout the Bible, deliverance has been part of the Good News. An example is the Canaanite woman who came to Jesus asking for mercy for her daughter who was cruelly afflicted by an evil spirit (Mt 15:22, The Message). Two gospel accounts (Mt 15:21–28 and Mk 7:24–30) recount that the daughter was healed and that the mother found the evil spirit was gone from her daughter. Driving out evil spirits and healing is included in Jesus's commission to His disciples and also to us. This includes stepping into the power and authority Jesus gave us over all demons (Lk 9:1). I look at this very simply: the root cause of all good is a good God, and the root cause of all evil is an evil devil. To bind, tear down, and destroy the entanglements of the enemy in a person's life is part of Jesus's ministry statement—caring for prisoners and captives by loosing them. Binding evil and loosing captives are all part of deliverance. "I will give you the keys of the kingdom of heaven; and whatever you bind [declare to be improper and unlawful] on earth must be what is already bound in heaven; and whatever you loose [declare lawful] on earth must be what is already loosed in heaven." (Mt 16:19, The Amplified Bible)

Binding renders an oppressive spirit powerless, which enables it to be effectively removed while protecting the afflicted from needless harm. However, if the vast majority of ministry is limited to binding and removing evil spirits and then not loosing and filling people with God's goodness, the outcome may be injured, empty, and frustrated people. To minister deep healing, it is essential to loose and fill people with the goodness of God as much or more than binding and expelling evil. One relevant scripture refers to the swept house needing to be filled or the state of the person will be radically worse than before the evil spirit first departed (Lk 11:24–26). Teach them to sweep their house clean and then to be continually filled with His presence. It is important to always fill the house as well as shutting the doors. Help a person be loosed and filled following deliverance by first blessing the person with healing of body, mind, and spirit. Also pray for the person to be filled with the Holy Spirit, God's love and forgiveness, and new life in Jesus. Then their focus can be on submitting to God, practicing new godly behaviors and attitudes, and resisting the devil.

Ministry

"But we recognize that *demons are like rats. And rats go for 'garbage.'* Garbage is the term I use to refer to the spiritual or emotional problems to which demons attach themselves."[1] Woundedness is an open door for the enemy to attack and afflict people. Because God has each person's vital information, we can ask Him for revelation of the root causes of the evil one's oppression. Then addressing these specific root causes with power and authority is an effective way to begin setting people free.

Assuming that every problem is a result of an individual's sin is presumption. It is fundamental to distinguish between demonic influence and the individual's will and flesh. Focusing on God and listening carefully to the Holy Spirit is essential to spiritual discernment. For example, just because a person refuses to deal with his or her "stuff" does not necessarily mean that an evil spirit is causing this unwillingness. The person may simply not be ready to be healed or ready to make the effort to change. The will and flesh can prevent cooperation with the Holy Spirit. Encourage the person to ratify God's work within by renouncing the world, the flesh, and the devil. Proclaim truth over the person to engage his or her will further. "For it is God who works in you to will and to act according to His good purpose." (Phil 2:13)

As part of the healing process, individuals should actively participate in their own deliverance as much as they are able. The Gadarene, with Legion (many unclean spirits), was able to run from a distance and worship Jesus. If the Gadarene was able to participate, it is not too much to ask others to approach Jesus and worship Him also. When people came to see Jesus, they saw the Gadarene fully clothed and in his right mind, and they were afraid, astonished, or awestruck (Mk 5:1–20). This eyewitness account of deliverance and healing is potent scripture. Darkness stampedes away from the Presence of light. As the person comes directly to Jesus, the Light of the world, darkness flees. There are no hard ones with Jesus!

Believers have authority to cast out all demons; however, it is also the individual's responsibility to fully renounce and repent of evil to be free. Willfully entertaining evil spirits (witchcraft, divination, sorcery, occultism, spiritualism, necromancy, etcetera) is strongly forbidden by God in the Holy Bible. Brazenly bringing evil spirits into the presence of Almighty God without examining oneself could invite devastation.

With a Word

We can minister like Jesus, driving out spirits with a word (Mt 8:16). "A word" in this passage is the Greek word "logos," meaning speak or spoken communication.[2] The passage immediately preceding Matthew 8:16, Matthew 8:5–13, involves the centurion, a military leader and a man in authority. The centurion used the same word, logos, when he recognized Jesus's authority and asked Jesus to speak the word and his servant would be healed. A spoken word with authority is not a request, a conversation, a teaching, or a counseling session. It is an order, just as an officer commands soldiers under his authority to execute a task. Whether in the military or in spiritual deliverance, a word is a spoken command. The clout that backs up our speaking a command with authority is God-given, and He expects us to use it (Lk 9:1–2)! Commanding evil spirits does not require a multitude of words in long conversation or extending grace for them to leave. Like Jesus, issue stern commands to evil spirits and speak the truth in love to people.

Set Them Free

The blood of Jesus and His broken body are the most powerful healing and deliverance tools available. For a person to be equipped to receive from Jesus both now and in the future, the person should apply the blood of Jesus and place himself in Jesus's stripes. "Set me free," "help me," and "have mercy on me" are prayers that get to the point of what is truly needed. They can ask Jesus to go deeper than ever before and do whatever it takes to cleanse, heal, deliver, and make them completely whole now. May God give us the spirit of wisdom and revelation to grow and minister more accurately and powerfully.

Doors

Jesus, *The* Door, opens doors of life and closes doors of death. The doors Jesus has closed for the person are as much a blessing as the doors He has opened for them (Rev 3:7–8, Is 22:22). Apply the blood of Jesus to permanently seal shut doors to all lies, evil, and oppression and then encourage the person to thank Jesus and go through the doors He has opened. You may consider sharing any of the suggestions in the appendix, "Keeping Your Healing," following this chapter.

Deliverance is neither a spectator sport nor a permanent solution to all of life's problems. Receiving healing and deliverance entails regularly fellowshipping with God and addressing hidden roots that He reveals. Each of us has personal responsibility as well as grace to continue living in and for God. A lifestyle of responding to God's prompting to transform us is crucial for spiritual health and keeping one's healing. This includes renewing the mind, walking in the Spirit, and addressing heart issues. It is indeed healthy to focus on the love, goodness, and power of God.

Prayer

Jesus, I open the door of my heart to You. Live in me. I am Your house, Your dwelling place. Reside in me. The Spirit and the Bride say come, Lord Jesus. Amen.

Post Note

My desire is that you encountered Jesus, His love and healing, while reading this book. Please feel free to fill out and submit an online testimony form at perfectloveheals.com. - Stuart DeVane

Appendix

Keeping Your Healing

*But grow in grace and knowledge of
our Lord and Savior Jesus Christ.*
2 Pet 3:18

- ➢ Live for God; love Him with your whole heart.
- ➢ Be filled with God and the things of God.
- ➢ Worship God and spend time with Him.
- ➢ Love and pray for your family and neighbors.
- ➢ Repent of sin quickly and sincerely.
- ➢ Continue growing in Christ.
- ➢ Hunger and thirst after Jesus.
- ➢ Seek first the Kingdom of God, and all these things will be added to you.
- ➢ Study, know, and pray God's written Word.
- ➢ Be good soil for the Word and life of God.
- ➢ Participate in a Bible-believing, loving, and anointed fellowship.
- ➢ Assemble together with the saints.
- ➢ Do something. Plant Godly seeds for a good harvest. Give out.
- ➢ Put on the full armor of God.
- ➢ Confess self-pity as sin; count your blessings.

- Focus on loving Jesus and others, not yourself and your problems.
- If you fall down, get up, dust yourself off, and advance on God's path.
- Look to Jesus instead of looking back.
- Pray to God and He will help you. Worry will hurt you.
- Give thanks. Don't forget all of His benefits.
- Share your healing testimony, both verbally and written.
- Jeremiah 29:11
- Go deeper in the basics as you go higher in God.
- Be filled with righteousness, peace, and joy in the Holy Spirit.
- Fellowship with God and receive His love daily.

Notes

Chapter 1

1. Dwight L. Moody, *D. L. Moody's Anecdotes and Illustrations*, Revised Edition, ed. Rev. J. B. McClure, (Chicago, Ill.: Rhodes and McClure Publishing Co., 1896), 12.

2. From the Strong's Exhaustive Concordance of the Bible.

3. Ibid.

Chapter 2

1. Timeless Truths Free Online Library, http://library.timelesstruths. org/music/The_Love_of_God (accessed October 10, 2009)

2. From the Strong's Exhaustive Concordance of the Bible.

Chapter 3

1. Timeless Truths Free Online Library, http://library.timelesstruths. org/music/Love_Lifted_Me/ (accessed May 28, 2010)

Chapter 5

1. Alan Redpath, *The Making of A Man Of God* (Old Tappan, NJ: Fleming H. Revell Company, 1962), 26.

2. John Wooden and Steve Jamison, *Wooden: A Lifetime of Observations and Reflections On and Off the Court,* (Lincolnwood, Ill.: Contemporary Books, 1997), 130.

Chapter 6

1. HigherPraise.com, words and Music by G. M. Bills, http://www.higherpraise.com/lyrics1/His_Name_is_Jesus.htm, (accessed May 31, 2010)

Chapter 9

1. Distinguishing the gifts of the Holy Spirit from the motivational gifts of the Father described in Romans 12:6–8 and the office gifts of Jesus described in Ephesians 4:7 and 11–12.

Chapter 10

1. Ana Méndez Ferrell, *Regions of Captivity,* (Ponte Verde, FL: Voice of Light Ministries, first English edition, 2009), 112-114.

Chapter 12

1. Charles H. Kraft, *Deep Wounds, Deep Healing,* (Ann Arbor, MI: Servant Publications, 1993), 45.

2. From the Strong's Exhaustive Concordance of the Bible.

About the Author

Stuart DeVane has been ministering healing for the past thirty years. He and his wife Shereen are part of the Healing Rooms and Apostolic Center of Santa Maria, California and lead the Healing the Brokenhearted Ministry. He earned a master's degree in counseling from the University of North Carolina at Chapel Hill and has worked in numerous social work capacities with at-risk youth and foster children. Stuart and Shereen live on the central coast of California and are the proud parents of two amazing young men, David and Daniel.

To schedule ministry or other training opportunities and for more information about the ministry of Perfect Love Heals, visit perfectloveheals.com or you may contact us at perfectloveheals@gmail.com.

www.ingramcontent.com/pod-product-compliance
Lightning Source LLC
Chambersburg PA
CBHW061150040426

42445CB00013B/1637